Feeding a Million in
Forty Days

Mike Housholder
with Merv Thompson

Feeding a Million in Forty Days
How a caring congregation
came together and learned that
miracles happen today

Copyright © 2010 Lutheran Church of Hope, 925 Jordan Creek Parkway, West Des Moines, Iowa 50266. No part of this publication may be reproduced, stored in a retrieval system, or transmitted by any means—electronic, mechanical, photocopying, recording, or otherwise—without prior written permission from Lutheran Church of Hope.

Scripture quotations marked NLT are taken from the *Holy Bible*, New Living Translation, copyright © 1996, 2004, 2007 by Tyndale House Foundation. Used by permission of Tyndale House Publishers Inc., Carol Stream, Illinois 60188. All rights reserved.

Printed in the United States of America
Perfection Learning®
ISBN 978-1-4507-0991-0

LUTHERAN CHURCH OF HOPE

www.lutheranchurchofhope.org

Acknowledgments

This book is dedicated to the great love of my life, Sally.

Many thanks to David Krause and Merv Thompson, who found a way to faithfully transcribe vocal words from a preacher to the written words of a book—not a simple task. Also to Gail "Radar" Smith, Chris Gunnare, and Lela Griffin, who helped with the details, as always, and for that I'm thankful.

Many thanks also to those who taught me that the church is better together, and that God does some of his best work through a coordinated body: Tom Housholder, Don Juel, and the amazing people who are Lutheran Church of Hope in West Des Moines.

Soli Deo Gloria!

Contents

	Foreword	vii
one	Walking Together	1
two	Reaching Out Together	23
three	Connecting Together	45
four	Serving Together	67
five	Growing Together	87
six	Living & Loving Together	107

Foreword

Feeding a Million in Forty Days is based on a series of six sermons delivered by Pastor Mike Housholder, senior pastor of Lutheran Church of Hope in West Des Moines, Iowa, during the Lenten season of 2007. This particular Lenten season, which we called Forty Days of Community, underscored how we are better—significantly better—when we work together toward a common cause and mission.

Ideas matter. Ideas motivate. Ideas inspire. Ideas transform. The Bible is absolutely the best place to look for creative and dynamic ideas. Jesus was the author of countless ideas about how the world could be changed and people could be healed. Just look at the parables and the rest of his teaching.

The problem we have today in much of the Christian church, however, is that we seem to be devoid of ideas. Or perhaps we've become stuck with only one idea from previous generations. New ideas and Christian imagination are essential in order for congregations to grow and thrive. Author Norm Shawchuck, who writes on church management, stated, "We are just one new idea away from transformation." I would add, "We are just two or three new ideas away from changing a whole congregation or community."

Forty Days of Community, an idea that originated with Pastor Rick Warren of Saddleback Community Church in Orange County, California, has transformational qualities. In the context of Forty Days of Community at Lutheran Church of Hope, this effort included the large- and small-group components present in Warren's Purpose Driven Life series along with an additional emphasis on service.

At Hope, existing small groups along with newly formed groups were encouraged to participate in some kind of service during the Forty Days of Community in 2007. These service opportunities offered outreach within the congregation along with outreach to the community and the world.

Of course one of the realities of ideas is that one new idea often leads to another, and then another. When Jesus says he makes all things new, this means that he helps us expand our ideas. Lutheran Church of Hope took the original idea and multiplied it manifold ways, leading to an incredible mission opportunity.

That new idea became a mission activity called Feeding a Million in Forty Days. Lutheran Church of Hope enlisted its membership and other worshipers to help create and distribute meals to one million hungry, needy people during Lent 2007.

The goal of feeding a million was chosen simply because it was so audacious, so impossible, so awesome, that two things held true if the project were to succeed: one, it could happen only through the power and grace of God; and two, the project was big enough to challenge everyone to respond.

Small ideas often receive small responses, but big ideas challenge us to make overwhelming responses. In the feeding of five thousand recorded in Matthew 14:13–21, Jesus wants to feed the huge crowd. The disciples have this pervasive attitude of scarcity, and so their advice to Jesus is to send the people away. But Jesus wanted to see how much food the people had brought with them so that they might share it.

The disciples found one small boy who had brought five loaves of bread and two fish. Jesus took the food and blessed it, and the food multiplied and fed the whole crowd. And miracle of miracles, everyone was satisfied, and there were twelve baskets of leftovers.

Foreword

If Jesus can take the food of one little boy and feed five thousand, imagine what he could do with food from five thousand. What kind of multiplication could take place right here at Hope? What is the sum of 5,000 times 5,000? Could it perhaps reach a million meals? That was the idea.

Feeding a Million in Forty Days had several components. In the first component, worshippers at Hope were encouraged to take home an empty grocery bag from the church. Seven thousand bags were made available. Those who took the bags shopped from an itemized list of foods. They filled the bags with groceries and brought them back to the church. The food was then distributed to several nonprofit organizations in the Des Moines area.

Lutheran Church of Hope also created a temporary storehouse on its property—a fifty-three-foot semitrailer with windows, heat, and light. The storehouse represented an important biblical idea: "Bring all the tithes into the storehouse so there will be enough food in my temple. If you do," says the Lord of Heaven's Armies, "I will pour out a blessing so great you won't have enough room to take it in! Try it! Put me to the test!" (Malachi 3:10). Of course in biblical days, the tithe was given in grain, so the storehouse became a place where people gave of their means and the gifts were available to those who needed the food—the poor and the hungry.

In addition, this onsite storehouse provided meals for those in the local community who were hungry. Soup and sandwiches were available to anyone in need. The storehouse was staffed by hundreds of existing small groups and groups that had just formed during the Forty Days of Community. So the first component was to help share seven thousand bags of groceries with the Des Moines community, which created more than twenty-eight thousand meals representing about 5 percent of the local population.

During Lent 2007, every person at Lutheran Church of Hope was challenged to be a part of the Forty Days of Community. Pastor Mike focused on this incredible opportunity during his sermons. Everyone was invited to join a small group for those six weeks so that everyone could experience spiritual growth, fellowship, and now service as well.

Part of that service, and the second primary component, was food collection and the campaign of Feeding a Million in Forty Days. Cargill Inc. and other major food processors had developed a particular meal to help curb hunger on a massive scale by serving populations in third- and fourth-world nations. The special meal consisted of rice, soybeans, and twenty-one essential nutrients tailored specifically to the needs of hungry, starving people. The role of members and friends of Lutheran Church of Hope was to assemble the ingredients for distribution as meals, and so the small groups devoted themselves to this effort throughout the forty days.

The cost of one box of food that held 216 meals was just $33, so we encouraged people to give one or more boxes. Give $33, and provide 216 meals. What an investment! As a result of this effort, more than one million meals were sent to Haiti, which is one of the poorest nations in the world. To achieve this goal, Hope partnered with the nonprofit organization Kids Against Hunger.

Feeding a Million in Forty Days was one of those transforming ideas that do not come along very often, although they do seem to come along frequently at Hope. This idea motivated and excited all of God's people at Hope and provided impetus for giving generously of time, talent, and financial resources. Lent is not just a time to experience the sufferings of Christ, but also to enter into the compassion of Jesus for the suffering of the world while doing what we can to help alleviate their suffering.

Of course we cannot do everything for everyone, but we can do something. At the time of the effort to feed a million, the membership at Hope was eight thousand. Now at the time of this writing, the membership has reached nearly twelve thousand and is still growing. And so we take to heart Jesus' words, "To whom much is given, much will be required." An attitude of abundance believes that Jesus can multiply the food today just as he did for the five thousand.

Let this transforming idea bring about new life, new energy, and new passion in each of us.

Dr. Merv Thompson
Teaching Pastor
Lutheran Church of Hope
April 2010

one

Walking Together

Two people are better off than one, for they can help each other succeed. – Ecclesiastes 4:9, NLT

God called us to an incredible journey during the Lenten season of 2007. None of us had ever been involved in such an exciting, challenging, transforming journey as we would soon embark upon. This vision was so unreachable, so over-the-top, so seemingly impossible that it could happen only through the awesome power and love of God.

The vision, and our goal, was to feed one million people in forty days. That's right—one million meals distributed to hungry, needy people during Lent.

As we anticipated this challenge, one thing became clear: None of us would ever have imagined achieving such a goal by ourselves. Which of us would even consider trying to feed one million people by ourselves? Who among us would dare say, "I don't need anyone else—this is just between God and me. I'm going to feed one million people on my own."

How preposterous that would be. If we work alone, we fail. When we go it alone, we'll be frustrated in our efforts. The goal of feeding one million people in forty days meant we had no choice but to learn we are better together—much, much better.

The Bible describes a powerful picture of the church when it calls us the body of Christ. The message is that all of the parts of the body are important—in fact, they're essential—and that all of the parts are designed to work together. When all of the parts of the body of Christ work in harmony, the body has life and health and unlimited potential.

When parts of our physical bodies are out of harmony, however, disease often results. At times, some parts of our physical body even work at cross purposes. The same is true in the body of Christ. When certain parts of the body are not doing what they were meant to do, but instead are trying to be something they are not, a breakdown occurs. This is why every part of the body is important. Every part has a dynamic, essential function.

This is why Paul writes in I Corinthians 12, "But in fact God has arranged the parts of the body, every one of them, just as he wanted them to be. If they were all one part, where would the body be? How strange a body would be if it had only one part." In other words, if your whole body were only a nose, your sense of smell would be highly developed, but you might have trouble walking. Or what if your whole body were an eye? You'd be able to see quite well, but how in the world would you eat?

So Paul writes these amazing words about the image of us as a body: "But God has so arranged the body, giving the greater honor to the inferior member, that there be no dissension in the body, but the members may have the same care for one another. If one member suffers, all suffer together with it; if one member is honored, all rejoice together with it. If one part of our body suffers, the whole body suffers."

The same is true within the body of Christ today. Every part is important. In fact what we have often considered the less important parts may actually be the most important. This is why Jesus says in Matthew 25, "Whatever you do for the least of these my sisters and brothers, you do it for me." Whenever we honor what the world sees as the less important parts of the body, the more Jesus blesses and empowers us.

Everyone's gift is needed

The reality of the body of Christ is that all of us have different gifts, talents, and roles, and none of us is more important than any other person. The goal of the body of Christ is that everyone would work together in harmony because we need all of the gifts God has given to us within the community of faith.

One of the tragedies within the church today, however, is that many of the gifts are often neglected. The healthiest body is that which uses all of the members, all of the parts of the body, and all of the gifts God has poured out upon us.

To achieve our goal of feeding a million people, for example, we needed every gift, talent, and ability in our congregation. There was no time for wondering why someone else had a different gift that was more visible. Rather, it was time to let God work through us as he empowered the gifts we *do* have.

At Lutheran Church of Hope, where we have a myriad of gifts within the body, it was as though we were looking for an opportunity to use all of our gifts together at the same time for a single purpose and goal. So the Lenten season of 2007 was truly the right time for us to come together as the body of Christ.

But this isn't how the church in America tends to function today. Over the past few generations, the biblical view of the church has often been eclipsed by opposing forces within society. Some segments of the broader church today have created something the apostles in the book of Acts might not even recognize as being "the church." This is because we've confused the essential elements of worship, fellowship, discipleship, and teaching. For some, church has become a place to come together for an hour on Sunday to sing a few songs, hear a message, say hello to each other, enjoy some coffee, and then go home.

But the proper image of the body of Christ is much different from this. In the true biblical picture, every member of the body needs the others. There is intimate, life-giving connection with one another. The Bible often calls this *koinonia,* a Greek word that points to the deep, abiding level of community, or fellowship, that we were meant to experience.

Jesus Christ is calling us as a part of his body to be in this deeper relationship with him and with one another. God wants us to be known, valued, and embraced by the rest of the body. But as our world becomes increasingly dependent on technology, we're actually becoming more isolated from one another rather than better connected. Instead of developing deep personal relationships, we're tempted to fall into what's called "cocooning."

As babies we were able to cry out and scream, and our mother would come and hold us. Now we often turn to Internet websites such as Facebook for human contact. Instead of actually touching another person, we send a text message on our cell phone. But that just won't do it. We need human community. It is the devil's game to isolate us, but it is God's will to bring us into community.

Stay in formation

Without community, without using all of the gifts and parts of the body, without working together in harmony, there was no way we could accomplish a goal such as preparing and distributing one million meals in just forty days. So the body of Christ needs to be the body, which is why each of us needs to enter into this community of believers and use all of our gifts.

When we're isolated from one another, we tend to be highly susceptible and vulnerable. We can be taken down and taken out. This is why, for instance, you see geese flying in a vee formation. Geese fly much better together. You hardly ever see just one goose flying across the sky. One goose is not going to make it very far. They need to fly together. I don't know all the scientific jargon, but geese cut down on wind resistance when they fly together in formation. When they share leadership and energy, they greatly improve their chances for everyone to make it.

Watch a team during a Tour De France bicycle race and you'll see the importance of working together. When Lance Armstrong of the U.S. team was winning all those races in the 1990s, the rest of the team helped him achieve those victories. The other bicyclists on the team would ride in front of Armstrong to reduce wind resistance, sort of like geese flying in formation. The team would draft Armstrong to the front, and then at the right moment, he would take off toward the goal.

Years ago when my oldest son was in the fifth grade, he and I participated in a bicycle ride sponsored by his school. We decided we would ride together and try to "win" the event even though it wasn't actually a race. We concluded the only way we could win was if we would draft, just like geese flying in formation. One of us had to get behind the other to provide protection from the wind, and then at certain times we would switch places.

I wasn't sure this would work, having never been a goose. But I wanted to experiment. And oh my, did it work! We were passing people right and left. Very quietly we moved up to fourth place, then to third, then to second, and soon we shot into first place. It wasn't hard to do, much to my surprise, because we did it together. When one of us would get a little tired, the other would get out in front and draft for the other. That's how you win the race, by drafting for the other person.

We need each other

Winning that bicycle race was fun even though it was just a game my son and I created. But being part of the body of Christ through community is not a game. This is about real life—*your* life. God has wired you with the need for human community. He planted within you a deep, abiding need for human contact. And even though our technological age seems to give the message that we no longer need others through community, this is absolutely false.

If we do not understand the biblical picture of the body of Christ, one of the temptations today is to pretend we are an island or a rock. And of course a rock feels no pain. It is too easy for us to say, "I really do not need other people. I don't need a group. In fact, I am an introvert and would much rather be alone." This is especially true for men, who are often the strong, silent type—the loners.

For those of you who consider yourselves introverts, you should know that I'm one of you. Publicly my calling as a pastor is to be extroverted, and so God gave me that gift for when I need it. But if you were to see me at home or behind the scenes or in small groups, I'm the quieter one.

On the personality profiles, I tend to be an introvert. I don't like parties—I don't know why people even have them. I don't like small talk or inconsequential chitchat. So this means I have to move out beyond my comfort zone to find community, to find friendships. I have to do this because I know that in the body of Christ, every part is important. Everyone must work together with every other member.

And more often than not, it takes effort to come together with each other in meaningful ways. In fact one of the common criticisms we hear of large churches today is that it's too easy to become lost in the crowd. Why not become part of a congregation, some will ask, where you can know the pastor and the pastor can know you and your story, and where you can know everyone else? On the surface this sounds good. The problem with this idealistic picture of church, though, is that no one can really know everyone in a church once it grows beyond about one hundred. Because we just can't know even one hundred people all that well.

Do others know you?

The biblical image of the church really has two dimensions. The first is worship, where the people of God, the body of Christ, gather to praise God. During worship the word of God is proclaimed, the Sacraments are offered, and the community of believers pray, sing, rejoice, mourn, and greet one another.

The second dimension is fellowship, or *koinonia*. This is where you are truly known because you are part of a community of believers—the body of Christ. And this almost always happens in a small group.

The character named Norm from the TV show *Cheers* that aired in the 1980s gives a good example of fellowship. When Norm walks into the neighborhood bar, Cheers, at the start of the show, everyone calls to him by name. Everyone is glad Norm is there, and that's why he keeps coming back.

I hope each of us has a place where we can find that kind of community, but of course a healthier place than a neighborhood bar. Because we all need a place where everyone knows our name and is glad we came, and in the church, that setting is the small group.

The Bible, in fact, is emphatic on the point that we *need* the small-group setting. When God created the universe and looked upon his work, he said it was very good. But when God looked at creation as a whole, he must have also said something like, "We have an issue here: The man is all alone, and that is not good."

When God was on earth in the person of Jesus Christ, he often needed to get away where he could be alone. So Jesus would go out onto the Sea of Galilee by himself in a small boat, or he would go up on a hillside to pray. At times Jesus needed a quiet place to be alone, just as we do. Yet in the midst of the thousands of people following him, Jesus chose twelve men to be his disciples. He also chose a small group of women to be disciples as described in Luke 8, including Mary Magdalene, Joanna, Susanna, and many others. So don't miss the point: Jesus was part of a small group.

And at those times when he really needed support, Jesus picked his three closest friends—Peter, James, and John—to accompany him. Jesus took these three men with him to the Mountain of Transfiguration and to the Garden of Gethsemane the night he was betrayed. These three men really knew Jesus as a human being because he needed to be in community. Just imagine: God in the flesh, fully human, needed other people through community.

And so Jesus sends forth the same call to each of us. He is asking, "Are you walking with other people? Are you trying to fly solo, or are you in formation so you can draft with one another?" Jesus must have gone through many pairs of sandals since he walked everywhere he went. But note that Jesus didn't walk alone; he always walked with other people. So again I ask: Are you walking with others as you go through this life? Are *you* walking as Jesus did? The Bible calls us to get up and follow Jesus, to walk as he walked and enter into community with others who are his disciples.

What does God want?

The number one question asked of those of us who are pastors is, "What is God's will for my life?" In other words, what does God want me to do? Here's the answer: If you really want to know what God wants you to do, you are going to have to get to know God. He is not going to post this information on a billboard for you. You are going to have to get to know his Son, Jesus. You are going to have to know the one who became human so you can relate personally to him.

John 1:14 states it this way: "And the Word became flesh and lived among us, and we have seen his glory, the glory as of a Father's only son, full of grace and truth."

The way you get to know God's Son, Jesus, is to walk with him and follow him. So how does this happen? How can you do what Jesus did, love people the way Jesus loved people, and treat them the way Jesus treated them? How can you get to know Jesus and hit your spiritual stride? The answer is to walk with Jesus. Then you will start to know what it means to be a follower of Jesus Christ. You will start to see God reveal his life to you.

But you cannot know this truth outside of community, outside of *koinonia*. You cannot reach your spiritual potential alone. If you try to make your journey a personal venture between you and God, you will never get there because God calls you into community through the fellowship of believers, the body of Christ. Remember that we are better together—much, much better.

Are you walking or waiting?

On my first day of school in the third grade, we had to walk past the sixth-grade classroom on our way to the lunchroom. I don't know what your experience was like in the third grade, but for me it was intimidating to walk past the sixth-graders. I was scared to death. They were a head and a half taller than us. They were bigger and stronger, and could squish us like a grape.

Walking past the sixth-grade class hadn't been a problem for me until that first day I was in the third grade. From kindergarten through second grade, we never had to go past the sixth-grade classroom. We were always on the other side of the building. Now that I was in third grade, though, we would have to walk past the sixth-grade classroom to get to the lunchroom. And just knowing that made me nervous.

But our teacher had us covered. As we filed past the sixth-grade classroom that first day of school, she just kept repeating, "We're walking, we're walking, we're walking, all the way down the hallway. We're holding hands and we are walking." And that's what we did—we walked and held hands, together. The teacher kept guiding us all the way to the lunchroom. Her voice was soothing, reassuring, and calming. We were moving. We weren't stopping. We weren't an easy target. And I wasn't scared because we were together. We were going to be OK.

What about your spiritual journey? Are you walking and holding hands with someone? Or has your spiritual journey become more a matter of hibernating and waiting?

Perhaps you aren't moving at all. You aren't walking but are pondering, thinking, and considering. If this describes you, then you need to know that this is not the way of Christianity. Because Christianity is something you do. It is *movement*. It's active. It's a place to go. It's walking with Jesus.

Start moving

If you want to get to know God, then you need to start moving. Start walking. Join hands with others as you start walking and loving people the way Jesus loved them. Start moving, and do it in his name. We are walking and following Jesus, joined together as the church, the body of Christ.

And because we are his body, we do the same things Jesus did. We serve the poor, we care for the oppressed, we reach out to those who are hurting, and we love each other. When we are in true fellowship we celebrate together, we suffer together, and we rejoice together.

And so we are walking together as the body of Christ. This is a movement, something we do, but it is not something we can do alone. Understand that the Christian walk is not between just Jesus and each of us as individuals. If you see your faith as just you and Jesus, walking through the garden, then you are missing some of the best stuff this side of heaven. Your faith *has* to be about you and Jesus and the world around you. It has to be centered in love.

As you go through this life, are you holding hands with others and walking in love? This was the theme of our Forty Days of Community back in 2007. Those forty days were an invitation, an experiment, and an opportunity for us as a congregation to learn to do a better job of loving each other and the world around us. We wanted to be more like Jesus. And to do so, we had to walk out our faith in community. We had to get to know each other better. In the process we discovered there were people out there who knew our names and were glad we were there.

Those forty days were not just about walking together, but also working together. Because together we discovered we could feed a million people in forty days. And together we discovered we could build twelve cabins at the synod Bible camp through our best imitation of an Amish barn raising.

So we are walking and serving where there are needs. We've sponsored mission trips to Ghana, Mexico, Jamaica, and other nations. Together we are walking and serving. We have volunteers who go quietly each week to work among at-risk youth or to serve at downtown homeless shelters. We have many who make local hospital visits or serve others through the Stephen Ministry.

We have dedicated Sunday school teachers who brave the cold and snow of the Iowa winter to teach the faith to our children. So we are walking, moving. We are not sitting around hibernating and waiting. Christianity is movement. By contrast the devil wants us to stop, to be alone, and to become isolated so he can bring us down. But don't stop. Keep walking and moving in fellowship with others.

Jesus says to follow his example, and the important thing is that you get into *some* form of small group. Become part of a community. Participate fully in the body of Christ. And it's not about being part of a congregation of five thousand or one hundred, because that is what we do in worship. Rather, being the body of Christ is about being part of a small group.

Read the book of Acts. The first believers gathered as a community of three thousand and soon grew to five thousand. In just a few weeks they mushroomed to thousands more believers who gathered in the temple courts to worship and praise God. But they also met in each others' homes. And in those days, most homes could accommodate only ten or twelve people. So the early church set the pattern for us as they met in small groups during the week and then gathered as a large group on the Sabbath. Every day they were walking with God.

So what about you? Are you walking with Jesus? Are you walking with others? Are you a part of a small group? Ecclesiastes 4:10 says two people are better than one: "For if they fall, one will lift up the other." Several verses later, the Scripture says three are better than two. So as you can see, it is much better to have people around you.

We all need community

I'm going to be really direct here because the challenge is so important. Some of you who are reading this are thinking, "I'm not really comfortable with all this talk of community, so just let me come to church and sit in my seat. I don't like being pressured to get into a small group."

And here is where I want to talk to men, and specifically introverted men because I know you. You're thinking, "I would rather *put needles into my eyes* than go to a small group. To have to talk about my feelings, to have to pray with people—I cannot think of anything I would rather do less. I just can't imagine sitting there sharing my heart with other people. I don't want to do that."

First of all, don't worry about it so much. Being in a small group is not all that intimidating. In fact there will be others sitting there who don't want to be there either. But you are going to discover it is not all that bad. After all, it's not as though someone were trying to talk you into something that is potentially painful, like going to the dentist.

Sometimes a small group doesn't work out. But if this happens, don't just give up. Because here is the problem: A recent study reported that on average, a man in our society has 0.7 friends. That's right—the average man has less than one genuine friend he can call. And not just someone he can call up and say, "Did you see the game?" or, "Hey, this is some weather we are having—do you want to borrow my snow-thrower?" No, I'm talking about someone who truly knows you, someone who knows your strengths and weaknesses. I am talking about someone who knows your struggles, someone who knows where you are spiritually. The average man has 0.7 people who know his heart, and that's sad.

We all have this need to be in community, this longing for belonging. We live in a world where it is dangerously easy to waste our time just staring at screens. All of this technology doesn't mean that all of a sudden we no longer need community, that we don't need each other. Because even if you are the biggest introvert on the face of the earth, God calls you to community. He needs for you to be in a safe place, perhaps with many other introverts. I know because I am one of you.

Just as we've seen through the life of Jesus, sometimes it is OK to be alone. But we also *need* community. Are you working with other people? Do you have people watching out for you, like a lifeguard who watches out for kids at a swimming pool? As the Apostle Paul writes in Philippians 2, "Do not look out only for your own interests, but take an interest in others."

Get into the game—please!

The first small group I ever experienced in a profound way, a Christian way, was my high school basketball team. I did not attend a Christian school, but our coach was a Christian. He didn't try to hide his faith. In fact he talked about his faith all the time. He talked about Jesus and quoted Scripture. This was rather amazing since it was one of the Chicago public schools.

We didn't realize what was going on at the time. We thought it was all about basketball, about winning and losing games. But as the season progressed my junior year, we began to realize this was about community. This was about love, about being the body of Christ.

There is a movie titled *Hoosiers* that depicts this scenario rather well. The team in the movie is made up of seven players and an assistant coach who tells the story of a team that wins the championship. Underneath the story, however, is a picture of love, of community, and of being a team.

There is one player in the movie that I can especially relate to because he is the preacher's kid, just like I am. During my senior year I was a starter, but during my junior year I sat on the bench most of the time. I usually got into games only when we were up by fifty points or so, or when the player I backed up got into foul trouble. I still remember how thrilled I was when I got into a game. I finally felt I was not just sitting on the sidelines but was now being asked to participate.

You may have spent much of your life on the sidelines, spiritually speaking. You may even be more comfortable there, more secure on the sidelines. But when you are called to go into the game, that is when everything starts to blossom. You are now being called to walk and move with God rather than just sit on the sidelines.

God comes to you through his living word. He walks right up to those of you who have been comfortable sitting on the bench, and he says to you, "We need you now. We need you to get up from the bench and get into the game. We need you to become a player."

This is what our Forty Days of Community was about. The body of Christ needs for you to get into the game. You need to start using your gifts and talents. You need to start participating. Remember that every part of the body is important—including you. Every member is critical for the body to function properly. So don't look out for just your own interests, focusing on what is comfortable for you. Look out for the interests of others, for the entire body. We all need each other. We all need to support each other, to love each other, to encourage each other.

Be accountable to someone

Let me ask you a question: Who holds you accountable? Who *demands* that you be accountable? Do you have such a person in your life? Each of us needs someone who will do this. We all need people who will come alongside and tell us when we have gotten off track. We need someone who will tell us when the way we are treating our family is off base, or who will challenge us when we are not being a good dad or mom or brother or sister. That is the purpose of community.

Do you have even one Christian friend who will come alongside and say, "You are not being good to your friends. You are pouring far too much time into your work. The way you are worshiping your career is not giving honor to Christ." Do you have someone like that? Do you have someone in your life who will say, "What you are doing is not good. What you are doing is not ethical, it is not constructive."

I challenge you to name those people in your head, right now. If your life has gotten off track in some area, is there someone who will tell you out of love that what you are doing is not good?

I have people like that in my life. I have three people in the church, in fact, who will tell me when my sermons are not good. I know they are doing this out of love because I'm married to one of them. My wife will sometimes come up to me after a service and tell me that I am going to have to change the sermon—that I need to "fix it." And I listen to her. I love that my wife is willing to do this, to confront me with the truth. It's not because she hates me, but because she loves me. She loves the people in the next service, and she wants me to fix the sermon for the future worshipers. So I love that she does that for me. (Of course I don't need for *everyone* in the congregation to do that. Because trust me—I hear about it, and I get it!)

So what about you? Do you have people like that who will come alongside and walk with you?

Understand that you need to be connected, you need community. I can't emphasize this enough. You need people who know you well enough to say, "This is not you. This is not who you are." People who are in recovery from addiction know this, which is why they continue going to twelve-step group meetings each week. They do this because they need each other.

The same is true for other people in divorce care, grief care, Alcoholics Anonymous (AA), and similar support groups. They keep going because people say to them, "You are not alone. We know what you are going through." They participate in such groups because in essence, people are saying to them, "We are watching out for you, we are watching you so that you do not fall back into the same patterns."

Can you see that as the body of Christ we are so much better together? We all need people who will lift us up when we fall. It is all about that AA sponsor who calls up a member of the group who might be tempted to drink and asks, "How are you doing today?" The answer then comes back, "I know you will hold me accountable, so I am not going to take that drink."

I want to emphasize how important it is that we have such support groups. At least 10 percent of the congregation at Lutheran Church of Hope is in some form of recovery. This is such a great blessing for our congregation and the community because those who are involved truly get it. They understand the need for a group and the critical importance of being in community.

But what about the other 90 percent of us who are not in some form of recovery group? We all have areas of our lives where we need someone to say, "What you are doing is wrong." Do you have someone who will be that honest with you?

Just as important, do you have someone who will encourage you as well as point out your shortcomings? When you are doing well, you need someone who will call out to you, "Way to go!"

Anyone who has ever run a marathon—which is 26.2 miles, by the way—knows the importance of encouragement. I have heard that at about mile 20, a runner often "hits the wall," so to speak. The body is screaming that what you are doing is not natural or possible, as though to say, "You must cease and desist *immediately* or I will shut you down!"

What I have heard that is most helpful to marathon runners when they reach this point is to have someone running with them. What they need is someone who will say, "Keep going—let's go just one more mile. Keep on running just a little longer, just around the next corner." A fellow runner who comes alongside often makes the difference between success and failure just by saying, "Let's just get to the next water station. Let's keep going a little longer. You are almost home, you are almost there!"

My high school basketball team lifted weights together. Our coach would tell us, "I do not want you to lift alone." He knew that together we would challenge and push one another to do more than we could ever do on our own.

Do you have this kind of Christian encouragement in your life? Do you have someone willing to walk with you, run with you, and ask the tough questions? Do you have someone that will say, "I missed you last Sunday. I didn't see you at our group. How come you weren't there?" Or someone who will ask, "How are things going at work? How are you handling the conflict with your coworker?" Do you have people like this who truly know you?

Our greatest need

Sociologists say one of the greatest unmet needs among human beings in our country today is that we are not known by anyone. No one really knows who we are. If you are really known by others, if you can name just three or four people who truly know you, then you are richly blessed. And this is not just about family. In fact, such people must often be outside of family because every family has some degree of dysfunction. So you need to find some sense of community outside of your family, outside of your marriage.

And while not everyone is married, the same need for being in community holds true for all of us. Single adults often tell me, and I hear their heart, "I am so tired of this world telling me I need to be married in order to be whole. I am so tired of all of my friends trying to set me up when I don't want to be set up."

Some single people are perfectly content to be single. It is who they are. It is how God made them. They don't need to be married to feel whole. If you are a single adult, perhaps you don't feel the need to be married. But you *do* need community. That doesn't change. You need people in your life who know you, who reach out and love you.

So whether we are married or single, we need people in our lives. But even beyond providing accountability and encouragement, are there people who would wait and weep with you when your life falls apart? Do you have people who would stand by your side during times of your deepest suffering? Perhaps you haven't yet needed such support. But trust me—at some point in life, you will.

We had a star player named Bob on my high school basketball team. After his sophomore year, Bob was offered a full-ride scholarship to Marquette University. He was voted onto the all-city team as a sophomore, which was almost unheard of in Chicago with its sixty-three high schools at the time and many players who ultimately ended up in the National Basketball Association. That's how good he was. As a junior he led us into the city playoffs and we almost won the title. We were a team, but we always gave Bob the ball.

But the summer after his junior year, Bob was diagnosed with bone cancer. His leg was amputated and his basketball career was over. Do you know where our team spent most of that summer? We were not on the basketball court. We were not playing in summer leagues. We were in the hospital room with our fellow player.

This was where I learned profoundly, for the first time, the importance of community. We were a small group, we were connected, and we were a community. In fact we were a Christ-centered community. Because of our coach, we did it together as one body.

Who's there for you?

If your life were to fall apart tomorrow, who would be there for you? I don't wish that upon anyone, of course. I wish that life would always be fair and sunny for everyone. But if you are going to live a full earthly life, there will be times when you suffer. You will not be able to skip through all the land mines of life; you are going to get hit somewhere along the way.

Those of us who live in Iowa know the weather can be good all winter. We can say over and over, "It is such a mild winter, it is such a wonderful winter." And then—wham, seemingly out of nowhere, we get hit by a major winter storm.

Life works the same way. Are you walking a tightrope without a safety net? Who would show up at your door tomorrow if your whole life fell apart? Who would show up who knows you? Who would be in a hospital room with you and stay through the night? Or sit with you in your living room for three hours and let you just talk through a traumatic event?

And especially important, who would show up and pray with you? You might say, "Well, my pastors would come." Yes, we would be there alongside you. We love to do this, and would be honored to be there. But here is the problem we face as pastors: For most people, we don't know you. We don't know you like God wants someone to know you because no pastor can know more than just a few people this way. I know the people in my small group, but I don't know them equally well. Peter, James, and John did not know all of the people in the church described in the book of Acts. This is why they got everyone involved in small groups that met in homes.

So who would show up? Who really knows you? Who knows your heart? Who would talk it through with you? Who would be there to wait with you? Who would weep when you are weeping? Remember that when one part of the body suffers, the whole body suffers together. The whole Christian family suffers. So again, who is going to be there for you?

John 13 says it this way: "I give you a new commandment, that you love one another. Just as I have loved you, you should love one another. By this everyone will know that you are my disciples, if you have love for one another."

Who is going to be there to witness to you? We need people. We need a Christian community. It is what God is calling us to be, to find people who will walk with us. God is calling us to find people who will hold hands with us. We need people we can know and who know us. We need others who will share with us and hold us accountable. We need people who will suffer with us and rejoice with us.

By living in a Christ-centered community, you are going to be an amazing witness to the world. It is your love for one another that the world is longing for. This desperate, lonely world has a huge longing for belonging. People are dying to find a place where they can be known. You can be a witness to them.

Your love for one another will prove to the world that you are walking with Jesus Christ. They will know you are Christians by your love. When you are doing what Jesus did, you have something the rest of the world does not have.

Lutheran Church of Hope may seem huge compared to some other congregations. We are known as "that big church with all those programs and people." But when you get inside, when you discover the community at work, then you know what the church is about. We are about love. We are about God's love and then, by following in his footsteps, sharing that love with one another.

The take-away for us during the 2007 Lenten season was learning to love better and follow Jesus more faithfully. Today we continue learning to know each other better so we can love the world better as well. It is not about what the world says we are, but who God *knows* we are and has made us to be. We are always better together, which is why God calls us into community.

two

Reaching Out
Together

Above all, you must live as citizens of heaven, conducting yourselves in a manner worthy of the Good News about Christ. Then ... I will know that you are standing side by side, fighting together for the faith. – Philippians 1:27, NLT

God has put each of us on this earth for a purpose. You are no accident, and this life you're living is not happenstance—God placed you here for a reason. One of the major themes of our Forty Days of Community that led up to Easter 2007 is the fundamental truth that God has put us on earth for some surpassing purpose.

And this purpose is not just an individualized, personalized, privatized journey that just you and God are on together. Rather God's call is for us to be together in community. We are better together, and God's purpose becomes clearer when we are together.

God has given Lutheran Church of Hope a specific mission to accomplish, and so there is also a specific purpose for each of us within this particular body of believers. In fact our mission statement as a congregation is a paraphrase of the Great Commission Christ gave before he ascended to heaven.

The Great Commission is found in Matthew 28 where Jesus gives this command: "Go therefore and make disciples of all nations, baptizing them in the name of the Father and of the Son and of the Holy Spirit, and teaching them to obey everything that I have commanded you. And remember I am with you always, to the end of the age."

The mission statement for Lutheran Church of Hope is similar: "Reach out to the world around us to share the everlasting love of Jesus Christ." This mission statement calls, guides, and inspires us in all we do.

We received this mission statement from God in 1994, and it has served us exceedingly well. The mission statement comes up in meetings, planning sessions, and teaching because it is such a solid reminder of what is truly important for us as a church. We know this commission to go forth was important for Jesus and the early church, and so we are on solid ground when we embrace it. In fact we believe this is God's call to the whole church, the Christian Church, and we are just a small part of that body of believers.

The mission statement is intentionally short and simple because we want everyone in the congregation to know it. We want our members to memorize it, to breathe it in. At the same time the mission statement is intentionally broad to cover everything we are doing, such as the work in Ghana through a small group of Hope volunteers under the direction of one of our pastors.

The statement is also lived out by those who go downtown to serve the homeless and through thousands of bags of groceries that helped feed a million people. It is for all of us who were united in the goal of feeding a million people in forty days.

It's really about being connected. Close to two-thirds of the congregation at Lutheran Church of Hope meet in small groups.

That means several thousand people are learning to be better together. I praise God for this incredible outpouring of commitment and faith.

If you are not in a small group, you are really missing something. You are missing one of the most important parts of being a believer. This is not to say you are not as good a Christian as those who are in small groups, but nonetheless you are missing something profound and life-changing.

Salvation, of course, does not depend on being in a small group. But once you have been saved and redeemed by God in Jesus Christ, how are you going to respond to his grace? What are you going to do with the new life God has given you? Understand that Christianity is more than just trying to get into heaven. Your purpose is to make a difference here on earth. And toward fulfilling that purpose, we're far better together than as individuals.

Abundance through relationships

I remember a conversation I once had with my dad when I was in the sixth or seventh grade. I said to him, "Dad, once we figure out we are going to heaven, once we know we are saved by God's grace, then that is all there is to it. We can then just live our life the way we want to live."

But he said to me, "You are missing the point. Christianity is not just about getting into heaven, although that is important. Christianity is about what we do on this earth. And not only that, but God is leading us to an abundant life he describes in John 10, where Jesus says, 'I came that you might have life and have it abundantly.'"

The abundant life Jesus describes is not the life the world defines. The world suggests the most important things in life are success, achievement, and receiving some of the world's glory.

The world's abundance is getting noticed and being in the spotlight. It is all about accumulating "stuff"—more and more money, things, and possessions. Abundance according to the world is power, prestige, and status.

But Jesus says this is not the abundant life. The abundance Jesus describes is to be rich in relationships and rightly connected to God. It is being connected to people that are connected to God. This is the abundant life people experience when they fulfill the mission God has given us. Our purpose on earth is to carry out the mission of God in Jesus Christ.

At Lutheran Church of Hope, we define our mission as a paraphrase of the Great Commission, that is, to reach out and share the love of God. There is nothing passive about that. In fact we can never become passive as a church. Our mission is to unapologetically reach out with the good news of Jesus Christ.

We have *great* news, in fact. And so we are not going to apologize for it. But neither will we beat people over the head with it, and we are not going to be careless in how we share that news. Hopefully we will find every way possible to more effectively spread the good news to our world.

For instance, if you had a cure for AIDS, wouldn't you tell people about it? If you had a cure for cancer, wouldn't you let somebody know? Or would you keep the news to yourself? Would you share the news with just your congregation and no one else? Would you develop a cure for AIDS or cancer but avoid telling anyone else who was not part of your group? That would be bizarre. It would be selfish and self-righteous.

But the fact is that we *do* have the cure for death. We do have the cure for all that destroys us in this world. God has given us his Son so that if we believe in him we will not die, but will have eternal life. This is the promise. But it is a promise not just for you and for me, but for the whole world. We cannot keep this kind of news to ourselves, this good news of salvation.

We have the key to a life that goes on forever. *We have the key.* We don't have the key to the cure for AIDS or cancer, but for something far greater and more valuable. And our mission as a church is to get out that word. Jesus says to us, "You are my ambassadors. You represent me in the world to get the word out."

In another passage of scripture, in John 20, Jesus says, "As the Father has sent me, so now I am sending you." This means Jesus is sending you out in his name. Many Christians, however, wish it were not this way. Many of us would rather have a personal, private faith. But that is where we get stuck, and that is why we never find an abundant life. We try to make faith about just me and Jesus, about what God can give me as though we're "consumers" of God.

But this is not why God put us on earth. He did not put us here just so we could get to heaven. He put us here so that once we have assurance of heaven, he can then use us for his purpose. And we can have abundant life here on earth only when we are walking in his purpose and carrying out his mission. That is the purpose for which we have been put in this place at this time, to be part of his mission.

Diversify your spiritual portfolio

How is this Christian life going for you? Are you reaching out to the world around you, sharing the love of Jesus Christ? Are you getting where you want to be? Or are you stuck in neutral?

This abundant life we're talking about is grounded in worship, fellowship, and community with one another. In the same way, the Bible clearly describes the life of the church. It is about coming together for worship in large groups, getting together in small groups for fellowship, and having personal time with God. And that is it: large group, small group, personal time with God.

Do you have a personal time with God each day? Are you spending daily quiet time with him? It doesn't have to be an extended period of time; it can be just five minutes at the start of the day. In fact it is good to start and end your day with God. During your quiet time, frame the day so that whatever gets painted inside that frame is OK.

When you have your quiet time, start with God. Talk with him. Listen to him. Read his word. If you need help getting started, find it. Many churches have daily Bible readings printed in the weekly bulletin to help keep you on theme and connected to the preaching. Many churches also include prayer requests in their bulletins, listing people in your church family asking for your prayers. And so there's five minutes with God right there. Or it can grow to fifteen or thirty minutes. The point is not the amount of time you spend, but whether you have a daily quiet time. Because without it, you are going to get stuck.

God wired you to be in relationship with him. He also wired you for worship—to sing his praises, to pray your prayers, to gather around the communion meal, and to hear his word proclaimed. This is our exercise as members of the body of Christ, to be together in worship and to the keep the Sabbath day holy. You can say you do not need this, but the truth is God wired you to need it.

Let me test you out on this: If you weren't able to attend a worship service some weekend because of a winter storm, like the ones we have in Iowa, would anything inside you not feel right? Would anything inside you long for something that was missing? Would you miss that connection with God, that Sabbath connection?

Understand that I am not talking about coming to hear a sermon. I am not talking about missing a particular preacher or the style of music you've come to enjoy. Rather I am talking about coming to the Lord's house. If you couldn't attend the worship service because of bad weather, would you miss being there? Would you sense a longing in your soul for something you were missing? If so, this is a good sign. It is a good sign if you would miss being among the body of Christ in worship on Saturday or Sunday. It is a good sign if you wanted more than anything else to be in the midst of other believers through worship. And it is a very good sign if all of a sudden you wanted to start coming to church, and you miss it when you are not there. That is a very good sign.

Here's how it should be: You come to worship because you get to, not because you have to. You join with others in worship because you are on the way to an abundant life. If you have a personal devotional life, if you have the large-group worship life, then you are on the way.

But even with personal devotional time and group worship, we are still missing the third dimension of the New Testament description of abundance: the small-group setting. We need the sense of community that comes only from being part of a small, intimate group of like-minded believers. And it is this part where many folks are still getting stuck.

The power of small groups

The other two components of the Christian life might be very prominent in your life—personal time with God along with large-group worship—but you must also have the genuine fellowship that grows only out of a small-group setting. If you aren't part of a small group, you are not going to have the abundance you seek. You are not going to have the fruits of the Spirit described in Scripture—love, joy, peace, patience, and all the rest. You won't have them because they come only from being together in community. The fruits of the Spirit don't just happen in isolation from others.

I want to make this clear: I am not saying that if you become a deeper Christian, everything in your life will become perfect and problem-free. I am not saying that at all, because that's not what we see in Scripture. I'm talking about a deeper peace *in the midst* of the storms. And make no mistake—storms will come. They never completely go away, but nevertheless God has promised we can find peace in the midst of life's storms.

How about you? Are you getting where you want to be? The genuine life changes that we all need happen best in small groups. This is not just our experience, but is also the biblical description in the New Testament. You cannot turn more than two pages in the New Testament without tripping over a small group. Jesus did it that way. He ministered in a small group. He sent people out in small groups.

The Apostle Paul worked the same way as Jesus. He called people together in small groups. You might be thinking, "But wait a minute, I thought the Apostle Paul went out solo. I thought he went out alone on all of those missionary journeys, because I remember looking in the back of my Bible and tracing the journey on a map with the colored line." But what is often not mentioned is that Paul *did not* go out alone. He was in community.

When Paul went to visit the early churches and create new ones, he established those churches in community. He did this through small groups. There are some verses in Scripture that we often skim over because we think they are irrelevant. But in fact these verses focus on the very truth of what God has called us to be and do.

Go to Romans 16, for instance. The book of Romans is an incredible theological treatise that God inspired Paul to write. We're told a man named Tersius wrote it all down. In verse 22 we see that Paul dictates the words and Tersius writes them down. And at the very end of the letter to the church at Rome, Paul mentions many of his small group connections.

He says to the readers of his letter, "Say hello to all my group members." Paul was saying hello to those who were leading small groups in the church of Rome.

And he doesn't stop there. In Romans 16:1, Paul writes, "I commend you to Phoebe, say hi to Phoebe." In verse 3 Paul says to give his greetings to Priscilla and Aquila, a husband-wife pastoral team that Paul had appointed to pastor the church. This verse is a huge challenge for anyone who does not think women ought to be pastors, because Paul appointed one.

In verse 5 Paul writes, "Greet my dear friend Epenetus." In verse 6 he writes, "Give my greetings to Mary." In verse 7 he says, "Greet Andronicus and Junias." And he continues with greetings to other fellow believers: Ampliatus, Urbanus, Stachys, Apelles, Herodian, Narcissus, Tryphena and Tryphosa, who might have been twins, Persis, and Rufus and also his mother, who Paul says was also "a mother to me."

Paul is saying in essence, "Give my Christian love to all these people. I was in community with them. I was in a small group with them. I love them as part of the body of Christ." Paul didn't do it alone, and Jesus didn't do it alone. I challenge you to find anyone in the New Testament who tried to go it alone; it is a very short list. They were always part of a community. They always carried out their mission in community.

Get unstuck

Are you stuck today? Are you not getting where you want to be and where God wants you to go in this life? Are you feeling trapped? If so, I ask you again: Are you in a small group? And if you are in a small group, is it a healthy group?

Let me broaden your definition of a small group: It is not just the group you sit down to do Bible study with. It is not just the group you gather with on Monday, or Tuesday, or Wednesday nights here at Hope, although that's great if you do and if it's working for you. A small group could be your section of the choir. Or a class you attend Sunday mornings before or after the worship service. It could be any number of groups.

As stated earlier, two-thirds of the congregation at Lutheran Church of Hope is in a small group of some sort, and in large part we attribute this level of participation to the Forty Days of Community emphasized during Lent in 2007. We praise God for this movement toward small groups because it has been such an awesome development in the life of our church. It is so significant that it bears repeating: The concept of being in community through a small group is not just another program, but a biblical description of what a healthy New Testament church should look like.

Are you hitting your spiritual stride? If not, it could be that you're stuck. And if you are stuck, it could be because you are not in a healthy small group. If you are in a group that is not healthy, I want to give you a prescription. And if you are not in a small group of any sort, I encourage you to get into one. This could be what is missing in your life.

Lost in the crowd

Let me give you an illustration. Do you remember Waldo, of the *Where's Waldo?* books? I did some research on Waldo. (It's amazing—you can Google anything these days.) And it turns out that Waldo is a loner, a recluse. And the reason Waldo ends up in all these pictures in all these books is because he cannot find a home. Waldo is looking for something in life that he cannot find.

Waldo is probably wandering around looking for life, and he cannot find it because he is all alone. Even when he is in a crowd, he is alone. He might have his personal time going with God, and he is just fine in a large crowd, in worship. But do you know what is missing in Waldo's life? It is the one thing that keeps you from finding him quickly in all those *Where's Waldo?* pictures.

And the answer is this: It's hard to find Waldo, or you, or anyone else in the midst of a large crowd. That's why the books sell, and that's why it's hard to find Waldo just by opening up a page and looking for him. You won't find him all that easily. No one does.

In the same way, it is difficult to pick you out in a crowd of a thousand people. So who knows whether you are in church on a given weekend? How many people in your church actually know you? How many people know your heart, your name, and what's going on in your life? Imagine what would happen if Waldo were part of a small group rather than just part of the crowd on a page in a book. It could still be the same picture. But within a small group, you could easily pick out Waldo from the crowd.

Do you see the difference? When you get Waldo in a group of seven, he stands out. But once you put Waldo back into the crowd and look for him, you wonder, where did he go? Waldo needs a small group so he can be known, so people can pray for him. You can't easily find him in a crowd, and neither can he find you. And yes, you need worship among other believers, whether on a Saturday night or Sunday morning. This is part of the biblical description of a healthy New Testament church, to be with the masses, the fellowship of believers. And you need a personal quiet time. But just as important, don't overlook your need to be in a group of twelve or seven or five, or whatever the number may be.

We've looked at examples from Scripture of both Jesus and Paul in the fellowship of believers through small groups. So there's no getting around the facts: *You need people who know you, and people you can know.* You need people you can pray with and join together in ministry. You need people who will check in with you often and who will go through life with you. You need to be able to rejoice together and weep together. You are church together. And always, you are better together.

Creation longs for community

All of creation reflects an overwhelming need for community. Consider penguins, for example. God created them with a need to be connected. It is not a want, but a need. Penguins were created to be in community with one another. In fact their survival depends on it. Note that you always see them together. If one penguin wanders off, he is dead. He is going to die.

This is a tough world, and God wired you up to be not all that different from penguins. You need community too. Consider that in the penguin world of the South Arctic Circle, so beautifully captured in the movie *The March of the Penguins*, the temperature is something like 80 degrees below zero, and that's without wind chill. The wind can blow one hundred miles per hour at times in the Arctic Circle.

Through this movie you could see that the lone penguin has no chance of surviving the severe winter cold. The lone penguin will simply fade away, absorbed by the great whiteness all around him. The tribe's only defense against the freezing cold is the group itself. It is almost as if they create another organism altogether.

In December, as the movie shows, the penguins are ready to leave the place where they were born. The younger ones have never known the ocean. They've never even touched it. But like their parents, they are of the sea. And so one day, for the first time, they will take the plunge and go home. But as the sunlight begins to disappear at the end of their fifth year, as the warm days begin to cool, they, too, will climb out of the water. And they will march, just as they have done for centuries, ever since the emperor penguin decided to stay, to live, and love.

To live is to love

The first time I watched *The March of the Penguins* I thought, well, that is the way of the penguins. But now it has hit me: To live is to love. If you don't love, you are losing life. God put you here for a purpose, and that purpose is to love people. You are here to love the world, to love people who are hurting, to love people who are lost.

The penguins' survival depends on love, and so does ours. We really don't have a life if we do not love. We turn into something God never intended. We don't have a life unless we seek community and participate in it. I am not talking about a community of five thousand, but rather a community of five or seven or twelve.

This is the way God wired us. Life is meant to be lived in community. If you have two genuine friends, you are richly blessed. You have community. And if you are blessed with that brother and sister kind of combination—and in the Church you have brothers and sisters in Christ—then you have community. This is the way God intended for us to live.

In Luke 10, Jesus says the harvest is plentiful but the laborers are few. Thus he chose seventy-two new disciples and he sent them out in teams, in pairs.

Note from this passage of Scripture that God never sends us out alone. He always sends us out in community. It is important that we worship, and it is important that we have personal devotional time with our Creator. Yet life-change happens best in small groups.

How many times have you heard someone say they experienced new life in Christ during a worship service? How many times have you heard someone say they found conversion, this calling, this deepening experience through worship? Certainly worship will start the process. But more often than not, worship will not complete it. Worship is always at its best when it leads into fellowship. It is best when it leads us into groups.

Billy Graham understood this from the beginning of his ministry. Whenever he arrived at a city for a crusade, he made sure that 75 to 80 percent of the churches supported his presence in that city. He never wanted to compete with local churches, but rather he wanted to support them. He knew that true life-change would take place in and through the local church.

So Billy Graham would give altar calls and people would make their march down to the stadium floor and give their lives to Christ. That has been an important moment for many people. Perhaps you were one of them. But if you ever answered an altar call at a Billy Graham crusade, you also know they pointed you to a local church. They always wanted you to find a place where you could be connected, where you could grow. They knew that worship alone was never enough; it had to lead to community.

Open your garage

Every Easter at Lutheran Church of Hope, we "open up the garage door," so to speak. Let me define this terminology. Living in West Des Moines, I've observed that when people open their garage door in most neighborhoods, they are sending a message to those around them that they are now "open." People are welcome to "stop by," as we say in Iowa. When the garage door is open, the message is, "Come on over. Let's compare snow-throwers. Let's have a conversation. Let's bring the kids along. The garage door is open, so come on over."

Maybe you're reading this and thinking, "Well, I never leave my garage door open." If so, consider the kind of message you might be sending: a bit standoff-ish, perhaps? When you open your garage door, you are sending the message, "Yes, we are in community here. We live together with you folks, and you are welcome here."

When the garage door is closed and someone who is a stranger comes to your house, they usually come to the front door. If you know them, perhaps they'll come to the side door or the back door. But when the garage door is open, this sends an entirely different message. And so Easter is the open garage door for us. We send out this message so everyone can come and meet Jesus.

One of the messages we give to those who enter through the garage door at Easter is that life-change happens in small groups. It happens in community. Thus we encourage all who come to the Easter service to participate in the Alpha course we offer. We emphasize Alpha as much as possible because it is in the Alpha course that genuine Holy Spirit life-change begins to happen.

Again and again we've heard this story: "Somebody invited me to an Easter worship service. Then I took the Alpha course, and Boom! That is where God nailed me! That is when my life changed. I will never be the same. I walked into the garage door and now I am sitting around a circle with seven other people, asking questions about life. And now look at me: I'm discussing issues of meaning and purpose and God and all those things. *That* is where it happened for me, in a small group."

Understand that such changes don't take place only within the context of Alpha. Alpha is not magic. Life-change can occur through any small-group experience. It could even be through a group of men that meet to watch NASCAR races together. We have such a group at Hope. Before the race they pray, do a study of some sort, and then they watch the race. That is awesome because that's how God works. He sends us out as small groups, in teams, to carry out the mission of his church.

If the church is to fulfill the mission God has given us, to reach out to the world and share the everlasting love of Jesus Christ, then it is going to happen in small groups. This is the only way it will happen. There is no Plan B. Because just as we were able to feed a million people in forty days, the only way this was going to happen was through small groups.

Do not underestimate the coordinated effort of a small group of people. Multiply that effort times the number of other small groups also doing their coordinated effort to reach out, and you begin to see the potential. Remember that Jesus started the same way, with just twelve unschooled men.

At the same time, consider this important point: Small groups were not created just for you. They were not created exclusively to meet your need for fellowship. They were not created just to make sure you are connected to the body of Christ, so that you are not lost in the crowd. Yes, these objectives are important. But understand that small groups were created by God and described in the New Testament as a way a Christian lives out a healthy life. It is the way by which a Christian finds an abundant life, for the sake of mission.

It's not about you

The small-group setting was designed and initiated by God. It was his intention that your group should have an outward focus rather than just an inward focus. God intends for you to be looking outward, that you do not underestimate what your small group can do.

Here's how you can tell whether your focus is inward or outward. If you are in a small group, is it always just about you? Is it always about your highs and lows, about your good times and bad times? If so, it's no wonder your small group experience is not as good as it should be. It *should* be about what you are doing on behalf of the world—those outside of your group.

Look at the story in Mark 2. There was a man who was paralyzed, and his friends wanted to bring him to Jesus. Only there was a problem: The house where Jesus was speaking was so packed that there was no room for them and their friend. So many people in those days were just like us. They wanted to meet Jesus, and they wanted to be in communion with him. But on that occasion, there wasn't room for even one more person.

So the four men who deeply loved their paralyzed friend and wanted to bring him to Jesus literally "raised the roof." They had a novel idea: They cut a hole in the roof of the house and lowered their friend into the presence of Jesus. This was a small group of men who were not inwardly focused, who just sat around in a circle all day sharing how they were feeling. This was a small group that reached out with the love of Christ.

When Jesus saw the man, the first thing he said was, "Your sins are forgiven." Doesn't that seem strange? The man wanted to be healed, and he was. But first, Jesus forgave his sins. Jesus was making the point that what the man needed first and foremost was spiritual healing. It was as though Jesus was saying, "I will heal you physically, but that is not going to last.

It will last only during your earthly lifetime. But the forgiveness of sins will last forever." Jesus first gave the man what he needed most: spiritual healing.

This was a small group that looked outside themselves and said, "We have a mission. We have a purpose for which God has brought us together. We are here in order to reach out to people who are on the mat." The men in this story thought they were bringing their friend to Jesus to be healed from paralysis, but ultimately they were bringing him to receive eternal life.

Think of the coordinated effort it took to bring this man to Jesus, to haul him up on the roof and then lower him down through a hole in the roof. The man's friends got very creative. But this is the nature of a small group, which is always more creative than someone trying to accomplish something alone. Groups are always more creative than solo performers.

We know this at Hope. Every worship service is planned by a group. Every single worship event is put together by a group. There is no way everything would fit together if I were doing all the planning. It takes a group. For our Easter and Christmas services, in fact, we have a dream team that begins meeting months ahead of time to plan and prepare for the upcoming events.

Small groups are always more creative than individuals. In the story from Mark 2, for example, the men knew Jesus could heal their friend and they knew their friend needed to be healed, so the challenge was getting the two of them together. The men must have shared ideas until suddenly a light came on: They could take their friend up on the roof, make an opening, and lower him down to Jesus. They had to use all their ingenuity and creativity, and they had to do it together. What if one of the men was more into himself than the group and had tried a completely different strategy? It would not have been a good day for the paralyzed man.

If they hadn't worked in a coordinated fashion, they would have failed. They had to work together. So again, do not underestimate what God can do when members of a small group coordinate their efforts. It was for the sake of mission that the group of friends lowered the paralyzed man to Jesus. And their ultimate joy came when Jesus said the words, "It is your faith that has made him well."

Faith and miracles go hand in hand. "It is your faith that has made you well" is what Jesus said. Read this again. It wasn't just the faith of the paralyzed man, but rather the faith of the small group of four friends that made him well. Their faith inspired them to take him to Jesus. They were on a mission from God. It was their faith that led their friend to healing and wholeness. Jesus was saying to the man, "Your sins are forgiven and now that you have heaven as your home, oh, by the way, get up and walk."

Let God work through you

What is your group doing for the world around you? What is your group doing for those who are "on the mat" like the paralyzed man? If you are not in a group, do you realize God is calling you to be part of one? Remember that this is not just for you, and it is not just about you. Rather it is about what God wants to do through you and your group.

God can do much through you as an individual. He can do much through us as a church. But God can do even more amazing things through people who want to coordinate their efforts in small groups. The church is not just growing, it is multiplying. Because when people join small groups, the church multiplies along with the mission of the church as people reach out to share the love of Jesus Christ. And it happens much more powerfully in groups.

Do you need to find a group? If so, why not start one and get others to join? Paul's letter to the Philippians says it this way: "Above all you must live as citizens of heaven, conducting yourselves in a manner worthy of Christ, then I will know that you are standing side by side." This is what glorifies God, that you are conducting yourselves in a worthy manner, side by side.

We are much stronger in groups. We sing better in groups, we reach out better in groups, and we do church much better in groups. And if you are in a group that does not seem healthy, here is my prescription: Start to pray for people who are not in your group, who are not in any group. Change the focus from you to them. Invite them to come. Listen to them. Love them. No wonder your group doesn't seem to have any energy; try turning your focus to people on the mat, and watch the transformation!

All of us know people who are on the mat, spiritually speaking, and perhaps even physically speaking. You know people who need to meet Jesus, to have their sins forgiven or to be healed. Start praying for these people through your group. Get their names known by everyone in the group, and work together to invite them. Focus your group on loving people, on sharing the everlasting love of Jesus Christ. If you are doing outreach as a group, you are using by far the most effective method of evangelism. You are carrying out the biblical mandate.

And if your small group is ailing, take a PILL—Pray, Invite, Listen, Love. This is the prescription for *dis*-ease. I have never seen a group take this pill and not get better.

The healthiest small groups are focused on outreach. Yes, they still share concerns and pray for each other within the group. They love each other and celebrate life together. They suffer and rejoice together. But they also know it is not just about them. It is about what God can do *through* them. So start praying for people who are *not* there in your group—people on the mat that all of you know, and then invite them to join you.

Have I made my point? *Get into a group.* If you do not want to join a group already established, start a new one. Be as creative as you want. If the groups already established are not as exciting as you might want, then perhaps you could start something like one of the groups we have at Hope, the Hope Quilters. Now there is an exciting group. Such a group is probably for about only 1 percent of the church, but then that's the point. We don't need this group to be exciting for 100 percent of the church, just for those who love to quilt. And this quilting group has another name, by the way: Stitching for Mission. They do this for a cause, which is why they are one of the healthiest groups in the church.

Start a new group

It is not hard to start a group. You just say, "Hey, I really like doing this. I'll bet there are some other people in the church who like doing this also." Then you call and find pastoral or church staff to help you. It needs to be a Christ-centered group, of course, where you pray and share and have a mission together. But you determine what common cause draws you together.

We have a motorcycle riding group at Hope called Hope's Angels. They are awesome. They pray a lot, which is important when you are riding a motorcycle. Each year they have a pastor come out and do a blessing for their bikes. They never let me ride, but they do let me bless the bikes.

We also have a group that is going up to the golf dome in town and golfing all winter long. If you are thinking, "Hey, that would be great," then start a new group based on your passion. What do you love to do? Chances are that in a church of nearly twelve thousand, which we have at Hope, someone else will love to do what you do. And even if you don't have twelve thousand people around you in the congregation, you'll still find others to join a common cause. But don't let it be about you; let it be about the people God is trying to reach *through* you.

What is God calling you to start? Maybe it is simply to invite people in your neighborhood over to your house. If so, you don't need a big group to get started; just three or four will do. You don't even have to plan anything except to get people over to your house.

This is the bottom line: If you are not in a group, join one. If you can't find one that fits, start one. And if you are in a group that seems to be going nowhere, get it back to health. Whatever the case, be a group that reaches out. Be a group that is not self centered and focused on you. Rather be a group that is focused on those who are on the mat.

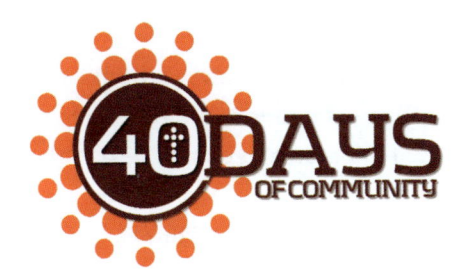

three

Connecting
Together

We are many parts of one body, and we all belong to each other. – Romans 12:5, NLT

Nothing in life is more important than relationships. In fact everything depends on then, and in our heart of hearts we know this is true. So much of Scripture warns against depending upon wealth or riches for finding satisfaction in life, and points instead to relationships as our source of fulfillment.

Relationships with God and other people are what truly matter in life, not our achievements or all the material goods we've accumulated.

Look at the design of God's "Top Ten" laws, the Ten Commandments. The first three commandments are about you and God. God warns us, "Have no other gods before me, do not use my name in vain, and remember the Sabbath day to keep it holy." The first three commandments are entirely about our relationship with God.

And the next seven commandments are about our relationships with others: Honor your father and mother. Don't kill. Don't commit adultery. Don't steal. Don't bear false witness. Don't covet your neighbor's house. Don't covet your neighbor's wife or anything else that belongs to your neighbor. All of the Ten Commandments deal with relationships, and the rest of God's laws focus on relationships as well. So this business of relationships is huge to God, that is, how we relate to him and other people. Why else would God use all Ten Commandments to drive home this point?

Everything starts with relationship

The relationships you have and the quality of those relationships are central to the abundant life Jesus talks about. This includes relationships between you and your friends; between you and your spouse, if you are married; between you and your kids; between you and your parents; between your brothers and sisters; and even between your enemies. We can't get around it. Our creator, God, wired us to be in community with each other. The Scriptures tell us we not only need to have strong relationships, but also how to develop and nurture them.

Most of the teachings on relationships in the New Testament concern how we relate to each other within the church. But the teachings are just as applicable to relationships within our families and our places of work.

How many of us can say we have perfect relationships with everyone at home and in the workplace? And how many of us need to develop *better* relationships? The truth is, we all need to know more about establishing and maintaining healthy relationships.

Self-help books and courses on relationships may offer some help. But many of them are fluff, and the effects of such efforts usually wear off quickly. We need something deeper and of greater substance than self-help formulas. And we need to consider how relationships are destroyed as well as how we can build them up.

The Bible introduces these concepts in Romans 12 where Paul writes that we are many parts of one body yet we all belong to each other. And this is the central truth: We belong to each other. We need each other, and we are better together. This is what our Forty Days of Community leading up to Easter in 2007 was all about.

As stated earlier, during that Lenten season we had two goals. The first was to learn to love each other better because this is a biblical mandate. The second goal was to learn to love the world around us by serving others, and we achieved this by feeding a million people in forty days.

What an incredible outpouring of generosity that was. Grocery bags were tucked in corners all around the church during that time. Literally thousands of bags of groceries showed up as people in the congregation responded together out of love to meet the needs of others.

During that time, I recall one of the local grocery store chains sent us a letter that read, "Dear Lutheran Church of Hope, the bags seem to be working. Please remind us of the items you're buying so we can restock our shelves." A woman in the church came up to me one day to tell me the store where she shops was completely out of some of the items we were buying. So I went to the store and asked whether they had a list of the items we were buying and giving to the poor. The clerk said to me, "Oh, you must be from *that church*."

Praise God for that! Everybody is known for something, and it was good to be known as "*that church* that has a heart for the poor." We know we belong to each other within the church as the body of Christ. But we also have a responsibility to serve and care for others around us.

Somebody else came up to me after the early service one day during those forty days and told me the local Wal-Mart store had run out of the same items. And that would have been just fine if we had cleaned out the items on our list from every grocery store in Des Moines. It was awesome to watch that happen. And of course there was no real reason for concern because the shelves would soon be restocked anyway. We're so blessed in this country. When we run out of something in a grocery story, we can always make more.

We even put a storehouse out in the parking lot. Because the biggest problem we had was finding enough room for all the food people had brought to the church. We didn't have enough room for all of the groups that wanted to help package the rice, vegetables, and nutrients so we could send them to starving people in Haiti. So we opened up the gymnasium and added two more shifts for people that wanted to help. We also partnered with a local car dealership that provided food for half a million people as we provided for the other half.

Haiti is the poorest nation in the western hemisphere, which is why we felt called to reach out and help feed a million people in that country. We hoped the movement would spread, that other churches would catch on and join in the momentum. And we plan to continue providing food and hope in the coming years because this wasn't just a one-time event.

Relationships are under attack

As the project to feed a million people demonstrated, we are so much better when working together than as individuals. We are so much better in relationship compared to going it alone. So if this is true, what causes relationships to break apart? And why do we allow this to happen? Our deepest satisfaction in life comes from the quality of our relationships. And thus the quality of life is at stake when our relationships suffer.

The number one enemy of relationships is selfishness, which is also the cause of most wars. Selfishness was certainly behind the terrorist attacks of September 11, 2001. And selfishness is behind most divorces. When a man and a woman start dating, they begin by courting each other. It's a play on words here, but most marriages that end up "in court" wouldn't have ended up there if the couple would have just continued "courting" each other.

During the early years of marriage, we might say to our spouse, "What can I do for you? How can I serve you? How can I give to you? How can I love you and meet your needs?" But then we fall into the habit of being selfish. And after a while, the temptation in a marriage or friendship can be to stop seeing the relationship as an opportunity to serve the other person and instead focus on ourselves. When that happens, we begin to ask, "What can you give me? Am I getting my needs met? Am I getting a raw deal here? How come you're not meeting me halfway? How come you're not doing your part?"

Understand that Jesus doesn't want you to meet the other person halfway through compromise. Rather he wants you to give *all* of yourself to that person. This means giving 100 percent rather than just meeting the other person halfway. You give all you have, everything you are, to the other person.

Two become one when you are both trying to out-give the other. That is when two become one. It happens when you are serving each other, loving each other. And so if you want to compete with each other, the way to do it is by serving and loving each other without holding anything back. By contrast, selfishness breaks down that oneness.

Rick Warren, who wrote the book *Forty Days of Community*, also wrote what he calls the five stages of a marriage using the analogy of the common cold.

According to Warren, during year one the husband says to his wife, "Baby, darling, I am worried about that sniffle. I called the paramedics to rush you to the hospital for a week of rest. I know you don't like hospital food, so I am going to have gourmet meals brought in to you."

Year two, the same cold comes back. "Sweetheart," the husband says, "I don't like the sound of that cough. I have arranged for a doctor to make a house call. Then I will tuck you into bed."

Year three, things are getting a little more selfish as the same cold comes back. "Honey, you look like you have a fever. You ought to drive yourself over to the clinic. Get yourself some medicine and I will watch the kids."

Year four, the cold is back once again: "Be sensible, woman. After you feed and bathe the kids and wash the dishes, you ought to put yourself to bed too."

Year five: "For Pete's sake, do you have to cough so loudly? I'm trying to watch TV here! Do you mind going in the other room? You sound like a barking dog."

Things can unravel pretty quickly through selfishness. It is so easy to become selfish in our relationships—with our spouse, our acquaintances, our coworkers, and our neighbors. The prevailing attitude of what you can get from another person is centered in selfishness.

So why do we treat each other this way? It's our human nature to do so, and each of us is a mess in this regard. We really are. We're selfish. We are sinful and unclean. By our human nature, we cannot live a perfect life. And if you think you *can* live a perfect life, I dare you to try. I dare you to go even one week without sinning.

Here's a thought: Try giving up sinning for Lent, for example. Just give it all up. That's right—no more sinning from the start of Lent until Easter. No more sinful thoughts, no sinful words, no sinful deeds. But good luck, because it's just not possible to totally stop sinning. Because of our sinful nature, we want to be selfish. We always seem to *want* what we don't have.

See what the Bible says about this in the book of James: "Why do you fight and argue with each other? Isn't it because you are full of selfish desires?" As James points out, you want something you don't have and will do most anything to get it. That's what causes problems. When we do anything we possibly can to get what we want, we destroy our relationships. Our actions tear our relationships apart.

Another translation puts it this way: "Selfish people cause trouble, but you live a full life if you trust the Lord." Our sinful nature, the selfishness that wants to know what's in it for me, leads to all sorts of problems.

A culture of selfishness

Along with our sinful desires as individuals, there's a second problem that leads to selfishness: We live in a selfish culture that is always sending messages that say, "It's all about you," or, "Have it your way." The message is always the same, that you know what's best for you.

Do you remember the ad for the soft drink, Sprite, which came out some years ago? "Obey your thirst," the ad said. Oh really? Do I really need to obey every little human, flesh-driven desire? Do I have to obey it? If I'm thirsty, must I obey my thirst?

Or how about this one—my all-time personal favorite as the worst slogan ever written: "What happens in Vegas *stays* in Vegas."

This is a lie, and you don't need me to tell you that. It's a lie and we all know it. Does this mean you can go to Las Vegas and commit adultery, and the act just stays there and nobody knows, nobody gets hurt? I can guarantee you it *does not* stay there. Because if you commit adultery in Las Vegas, you'd better believe you take it with you when you go back home.

Or if you go to Las Vegas and gamble away your family's inheritance or your life savings, your nest egg, I guarantee you—well, I guess in this case it *does* stay there—but you will bring it back nevertheless. Because unlike the ad says, what happens in Vegas never just stays there; you're going to carry it with you. You must carry the guilt or the shame or the burden or the outcome or the problem that comes from whatever it is you've done. So make no mistake—whatever it is you think you might get away with, whether in Las Vegas or elsewhere, it *never* just stays there.

What a selfish perspective—to think I can do whatever I want, that I can follow my own desires with no consequences for my actions. The Bible is filled with passages of scripture on this topic, especially in the New Testament. When Paul writes to the church he is saying, "You know, you've got a battle going on here." And there is indeed a battle going on: the flesh versus the spirit.

Headed for a crash

Let me ask you this: Who gets the most attention in your life? Is it you—the desires of your flesh, whatever those may be? If so, if you find yourself obeying your thirst, that is, your human desires, doing whatever you feel like doing, then I guarantee you're going to crash. If you live your life this way, you are on your way toward destroying your relationships.

When God sees us living this way, though, he says to us, "I am not mad at you. I am just brokenhearted. I'm calling you back because I have created you to be in relationship with me and other people." Understand that you cannot have lasting relationships if life is all about you, about merely satisfying your wants and needs. Because if life is only about your feelings, about getting your needs met, you are going to die. You will end up lonely, bitter, and broken because selfish people cause trouble for themselves and others.

A full life comes only as we begin telling the truth about ourselves to the Lord. What is the focus of your life? Do you live for the spirit, or the flesh? Do you tend to say, "Well, God, you created me, you created the world, you created me with the need for community, and I know relationships are important to you. But I am going to ignore you. I am going to ignore what you say about living in relationships. Instead I am going to create my own set of rules. I am going to do it *my way*."

If this is how you've been living, how is it working for you? What has been the outcome? What is the product of living life your way instead of God's way? How good are your relationships? How strong, deep, and lasting are they? Are you able to say, "My friends stay around for years—for decades, in fact. I have relationships that last." If you can say this, it is probably because you are living God's way. It is because there is more selflessness than selfishness in your life.

We reap what we sow

Philippians 2:4 says, "Let each of you look not to your own interests, but to the interests of others." Galatians 6:7 says, "You reap what you sow. If you sow to the flesh, you will reap corruption from the flesh. If you sow to the spirit, you will reap eternal life from the Spirit. So then whenever we have opportunity, let us work for the good of all, and especially for those of the family of faith."

You reap what you sow. Remember this. Because if you plant criticism, you will get criticized. If you plant gossip, you will receive gossip. So don't be surprised—if you plant hatred, people are going to hate you. But if you plant love, people are going to love you. Because the more we hang out with people, the more we also begin to sound like them, talk like them, and behave like them.

But Jesus comes along and says to us, "I would like for you to really know who I am. I would like to be friends with you. I would like for you to hang out more with me." What does this really mean? This means that Jesus wants us to be reading his word. It means he wants us to be talking to him in prayer. It means he wants us to hang out with him through worship.

And it means Jesus wants us to serve him. He says to us, "I want you to follow me. I want you to love people the way I have taught you to love. And not just with words, but by your example. I want you to follow in my footsteps. I want you to learn how to live your life the way I lived mine."

This is following the leader. Because the more we do this, the more we follow the pattern Jesus gave us, the more satisfying our lives will be, the richer our relationships will become, and the more full our spirits will be.

We reap what we sow. And so if we live our own sinful life by our own set of morals, we will harvest a life of decay and death. We will be doing the very things that suck the life out of us. God is life and this Creator of life says to us, "I want to give you life." But even so, God will let us go our own way if that's what we choose. He will not protect us from the consequences of creating our own moral path.

Jesus says, "I want you to have life, and I want it to be abundant. I want it to be full. So live to please me. Live to follow me. Follow my example. Live life the way I did and you will be full. Because whatever you sow you will also reap."

In other words, love others. Jesus sums up all the commandments with just this one word, love. Throughout Scripture Jesus is saying, "Just love people the way I love you. Do as I did, loving people the same way. Put others first. Be selfless, not selfish."

The problem with pride

As we've seen, selfishness destroys relationships. And the second destructive force is pride, which is all about our egos. Think of the word ego as standing for "Edging God Out." Because this is what happens when the ego dominates. We push God out of the way. We are so full of ourselves that there is no room to be filled by the Spirit. The Bible says, "Pride leads to conflict, but those who take advice are wise."

The more familiar verse regarding pride comes from Proverbs 16:18, "Pride comes before the fall," in the English translation of the original Hebrew. And it's true—pride does come before the fall. Pride shows up in all sorts of ways. It's a surface issue for some folks that say, "I'm proud that I don't have any pride issues." But if you are a critical person, this is probably a sign that pride is the root problem.

Pride is much like a tsunami, a giant wave that destroys thousands of lives when it finally hits a coast somewhere around the world. But it isn't really the wave itself that brings death and destruction. The cause is actually an earthquake somewhere out in the ocean.

In the same way, we sometimes focus on the wave and the destruction it causes in our life rather than searching out the root cause, the earthquake. Because it's not the critical spirit you might have that is the problem, but rather the problem is the pride that causes you to have that spirit. So you're going to have to deal with the pride before you can stop criticizing people. You are going to have to learn to humble yourself and let go of pride. Ultimately you're going to have to stop acting as though you are perfect.

If you are competitive by your sinful nature, always comparing yourself to others—whether comparing your clothes, car, spouse, family, career, income, or even where you take your vacation—then the issue behind it is pride. Because if you think "winning" or "losing" in life is based on such things, the issue is not competitiveness, but pride. If you have what looks like stubbornness on the surface, the deeper root cause is probably pride.

And here's how you can tell: Is it hard for you to admit you're wrong? There are people like this all around us, people who are never wrong. If you grew up Lutheran, in fact, you probably knew people like this. Remember your grandpa? Or maybe your aunt, the one who looked like the church lady, who was never wrong?

If you can be honest with yourself, perhaps you're in that same place. For example, when was the last time you could acknowledge the truth and say the words, "I was wrong," and you weren't just saying the words as a cop-out to get out of a bad situation, but you truly meant it? When was the last time you said something like this from the heart?

Can you say the words, "I was wrong. I am sorry. Please forgive me."? Or do you find yourself thinking this is what weak people say? No, this is what *honest* people say. On the other hand, pride and stubbornness often become an excuse. Pride often says, "I am a rock. I am strong. Yes, I have a lot of stubbornness. But I am proud of it, and I'm not going to change."

If this is you, then you need to start being honest with yourself. You're living in self-deception. You are pretending to be perfect. But who could ever be perfect? You may act as though you're never wrong. So if this is you, if this is how you see yourself, what an amazing person you must be, to never be wrong.

I hope you can think of a time over the past week when you were honestly able to say to someone, "I'm sorry. I was wrong. Please forgive me." Because the truth is, you are *not* perfect—none of us is. And the people who truly love you do not need for you to be perfect. And if they do, then they're the ones that have issues.

People will love you just for who you are—the real you. And you would be a whole lot better to hang out with if you would just come clean, if you would acknowledge the truth about yourself. To be able to say "I messed up" can be truly freeing.

Blessed are the humble

The opposite of pride is humility, which allows us to use our part in life to fit into the whole. And it's not that hard to tell whether we're humble or proud. Ask yourself this: Is life always about you? Or are you making sure you blend in with others?

A popular music group from the 1960s, the Temptations, recorded a number of hits, including the popular song "My Girl." They sang with such grace and amazing harmony. In fact they were known primarily for their vocal harmony. All of their biggest hits happened quickly.

But then David Ruffin, the lead singer in the Temptations, had a problem with pride. He noticed that a female vocal group popular at the same time, the Supremes, became known as Diana Ross and the Supremes. David Ruffin decided he wanted the same thing for himself. Just being a member of the Temptations was no longer enough; he thought the group should be renamed *David Ruffin* and the Temptations.

David Ruffin was no longer content to be part of the whole, and this became a problem. "I want to be the man," he was saying in essence. "I want to be the one in the spotlight, the one who gets all of the attention. I don't want to blend in anymore. I don't want to watch the director anymore. I don't want to follow along and make sure my voice blends with all the others. I want to be number one—they should serve *me*."

But David Ruffin got it backwards, and soon the famous singing group fell apart. A version of the Temptations continued to perform, but the group would never be the same.

The same thing happened to the famous 1960s band The Beach Boys. Pride got in the way. There are now three different versions of The Beach Boys touring the country. They should be honest and call themselves "The Beach *Boy*" and a bunch of friends because that is what each of these former band members has become. And pride is to blame. Because each of them insists, "I am the reason The Beach Boys were so big." That is what pride does to us.

Our me-first mentality

Does this sound at all like you, like your relationships with other people? Does life always have to be about you? Humility takes the opposite attitude. Humility says it is not just about you. Humility insists on "you first" rather than "me first" as your attitude. In relationships, humility cares more about the other person than you care about yourself.

God loves you, which is why the Bible tells us to sympathize with each other. To love each other as brothers and sisters. And to be tender-hearted toward one another. My way of reading this says it is the humble attitude that allows you to be sympathetic. It allows you to love people as brothers and sisters, and it allows you to be tender-hearted.

If you don't have humility, it is not simply going to come to you. Humility is the antidote to pride, which comes out in all sorts of ways, even in small groups. If you are in a small group and it is not going so well, which can happen, maybe it is because of pride. As much as God wants us to work together as a coordinated body, sometimes even our small groups become discordant. And do you know why? It's because we are human and sometimes pride and selfishness take over.

If you're in some sort of small group in your church, then you're bound to have one or more "EGRs" in your group. The letters "EGR" stand for "Extra Grace Required." You know the type—these are the folks that are hard to love. If no one comes to mind as an EGR in your group, well, perhaps it's because the EGR in the group is *you*.

Test yourself out on this: When you are in your small group and are listening to someone tell a story, are you tempted to not listen? Are you tempted to mentally wander off and think to yourself, "I can't *wait* for this person to shut up so I can top his story. I can see his story is going to be about how his kid got some kind of award. But I'm going *raise* him two. Because my kid got that same award plus two other things, so watch this..." If this is your tendency, the problem is pride. And you are the one with the pride.

Or perhaps you're in a small group and always offer advice, but never ask for any. You are always there to fix everyone else in the circle, but you're never ready to listen. You just cannot understand that someone could have a word for you, a word from God. Or pride can lead you to never admit you have any problem at all, so you never let people get close to you.

What are we afraid of?

The third destructive behavior along with selfishness and pride, and which a lot of us have in our relationships, is insecurity. That's right—insecurity. It is the kind of insecurity that is based on fear—the fear of allowing others to get too close. Because I am afraid that if you get too close, then I will be exposed for who I really am. And if you truly know me, then you will reject me.

For some people there is good reason to feel this way, because this is the way they were raised. When you were growing up, perhaps you had no one to model good, safe relationships. Your family may have been full of secrets, where no one could be honest with each another. And if so, this is an issue you're going to have to work through.

But God can work through this with you. God can work it through so you can drop the barriers and tear down the walls. God can work it out so you will begin to allow people to come close to you, because you need that closeness. You need that in your life.

You might be thinking, "Well, keeping people at arm's distance allows me to breathe, it allows me to live." But what you are missing is that God wired you up to *need* to be known by others, not to live at arm's length from them.

You cannot be known if you are always pushing people away. Because not only do you need to love other people, but you need to be loved by others. You need to have somebody, or better yet, two or three people in a group who truly know you. You need to have a spiritual partner, someone you can walk with. I am not referring to a marriage here, but a brother or sister in Christ.

Every man needs another man that will walk through this life with him, and every woman needs another woman who truly knows her. All of us need someone who is an equal, someone to just come alongside who knows us, where we can drop our boundaries and let them in. We all need to be loved, and we all need to be known.

Be honest with yourself: Do you have somebody like this in your life? Do you have someone who knows you even better than you know yourself? You may say, "No, I don't need that. I like my privacy." But that is fear doing the talking; you don't want anyone to get that close, so you don't let them in.

Risk loving, being loved

The Bible has much to say about this matter of fear, of not allowing ourselves to get too close to others. I am not talking about getting close to people who might hurt us, but to people we can trust. I am talking about finding a brother or sister in Christ, a genuine soul mate. Finding a person you can trust, a person you can come this close to, is God's will. Fear of that closeness disables us. But trusting in God protects us and gives us life. The antidote to insecurity is love.

In recent years a story circulated on the Internet about a man named Dick Hoyt whose son, Rick, is in a wheelchair. Rick Hoyt was born in 1963 with the umbilical cord wrapped around his neck, which caused numerous serious health problems. Nine months after Rick was born, the doctors told his parents, "You really should institutionalize your son. He is never going to be able to walk. He can't really think, and there is nothing going on in his mind."

But Dick Hoyt disagreed with the doctors. He saw something in his son that no one else saw. And by the time Rick was in high school, technology had reached the point where it was possible to create a device through which Rick could use the side of his head to type messages. And so he started communicating with the world around him, and in fact he turned out to be a bright student.

While Rick was in high school, one of his classmates was stricken with cancer, and a charity run was planned on behalf of the student. And even though he was in a wheelchair, Rick decided he wanted to participate in the charity run. But to do so, he would need his father's help. Now Rick's dad was in no shape to run a 5K race, but for the sake of his son, the dad dropped his insecurity and took the risk of joining the race. And so along with his son, Dick Hoyt ran the race. And then he ran again. And again. Love is a risk. Love is always a risk.

Now the father and son run every weekend. Dick Hoyt is in his sixties. They applied for the Boston Marathon and started running that race in 1979. The best time they turned in is just 42 minutes off the Olympic record. *42 minutes.* Imagine what it would be like for a twenty-five-year-old man running the Boston Marathon when along comes a sixty-year-old guy pushing his adult son in a wheelchair and he asks you, "How's it going?" and then passes you by.

That is the power of love. Rick and Dick Hoyt have now competed in 212 triathlons where they run, swim, and bike together. They have done five ironman triathlons. That is the power of hope. The father saw something in his son, and he chose to come close. He chose love. And love is a choice.

But you know this, right? Most people get it wrong. Most people think love is a feeling, but it's not. No, love is a choice that *produces* feelings. Love is not a feeling that you have to choose. Love is a choice. Make the choice to love and it will produce great feelings within you, and great emotion. Rick Hoyt recently wrote, "My big dream in life is one day for my dad to be in the wheelchair and for me to push him." That's love.

What this father and son have makes them rich. I have no idea how much money they make or how much income they have. But they are two of the richest men on the face of the earth. Do you know why? They have learned to love.

This is what God is trying to teach all of us. He says, "I want to teach you how to love." This is where life is to be found: in love. This is where the richness is. This is where the blessings are, where the benefits are. Life is not found in achievements. Life is not to be found in the size of your house or in the awards you receive. Life is not about the things we get in life, even though such things are just fine. They just are not going to fill you up.

Choose life, choose love

Life is about relationships. It is love. And love is that which gives you life. Where you don't have love, you don't have life. Choose life, God says. Choose love. And remember, you reap what you sow. Are you planting love? Or are you planting hatred? Are you getting mad at the world for not loving you back? Relationships are built through selflessness over selfishness. Humility over pride. Love over insecurity. Forgiveness over resentment.

Get rid of resentment in your life. It is toxic, and it destroys relationships. It is so easy to be offended in this world. People do offensive things, and nobody is immune. If we are human, we are going to get offended. But what God is interested in is how you handle such treatment. Are you the kind of person who, when offended, sort of flips out and dismisses that person from your life? If so, God says, "You are dying. You are dying in your resentments." Let it go. Learn to forgive, learn to love.

When Sally and I were married, Sally's grandmother—Grandma Gert, she's called—was at our wedding. Grandma Gert is a happy, vibrant, vivacious person, and Sally naturally comes by that same personality. But Grandma Gert had one disturbing issue in her life. When Sally and I got married in 1987, Grandma Gert had not talked to her sister, Aunt Edna, for ten years. They went for an entire decade without speaking to each other.

I asked Sally what had caused them to not talk for ten years. But Sally didn't remember. You know, these resentments are usually pretty trivial. They usually don't amount to much, but still we often hold onto the grudge, we hold onto the anger. We say to ourselves, "You have done me wrong, and I am never going to forgive you. I am never going to let it go."

What a horrible position to put yourself in. God says it is like putting yourself in a prison. Every day of your life, you are just binding yourself up with chains. You refuse to let go. Don't misunderstand; I am not talking about saying to a person who treated you badly, "It is OK." Forgiveness does not mean blessing the hurtful behavior of another person. It does not mean you are condoning it, and it does not mean what they did to you was right.

Unload your pain

From a biblical standpoint, forgiveness means, "I am making a choice to no longer carry this pain. I am letting it go. I am making a choice to let go of my right to get this person back. I am letting go of my right to get revenge on this person."

"Vengeance is mine," says the Lord. And the Lord is saying to you, "Let me take care of the justice issues. It will all come out in the wash. *You* work on forgiveness."

Romans 12 says, "As far as you are able, live at peace with everyone around you." Make sure you have done everything you can to make peace. Forgiveness means letting go of the pain, which many of you are carrying because you cannot forgive. Forgiveness means letting go of the right to take revenge, to retaliate against another person. It's our human nature to say, "You did me wrong, and so now I am going to do *you* wrong, only a little bit worse."

But God says we have to let it go. "It is because I love you," God says, "that I want you to have a life, and an abundant life. But you will never have that kind of life as long as you are holding onto grudges. So let me set you free from that."

We might say in response, "Sorry, but I don't have the power to do that. I don't have the will to be able to let go of the pain." But God says to us in Colossians 3, "Let me inspire you to let it go. Let me give you a reason to let it go. Make allowances for each other's faults, and forgive anyone who offends you." Remember, the Lord forgave you, so you must forgive others.

Even so you might still argue, "But I don't have the will to forgive everyone who has offended me. There are people who have done things to me that are so wrong, so unjust. It is unrighteous, some of the things that have been done to me."

I have a list like that, and I am sure you do too. We all have a list of people who have done us wrong. There was no rhyme or reason to what they did to us. It was just malicious. It was hateful. But let it go. Talk to that person today if you need to, if you can. Or call the person. But whatever you do, let it go. Let go of it in your heart. Talk to God about it, and just let it go.

Leave it at the cross

Where do we get the inspiration to do this? I don't have the will to do it, and so God leads me to his cross. He forces me to look at the cross, forces me to remember why he went to the cross on my behalf. The cross reminds us of God's grace, which we desperately need. It reminds us of how much God loves us.

God loves you so much, in fact, that he gave his Son, and there on the cross his Son looks out at you, the offender, the one who put him there. And he says to you and to me, "Father, forgive them for they don't know what they are doing."

Forgive the people in your life that have hurt you. I have forgiven those people in my life. So let it go. Remember that the Lord forgave you, so you must also forgive others. Learn to let it go.

Who is it that you still need to forgive? Who is it that you need to take the risk to learn to love? Who is it that you need to be more humble with? Who is it with whom you must be more selfless instead of selfish?

Maybe it is time for you to renew your marriage or your family relationships. Maybe it is time for you to start reaching out to those people the same way Jesus reached out to you. Forgive them the way he forgives us. You cannot forgive them on your own, but God says he will give us the power to do it.

God says, "I will give you the will to do it. I will give you the means to do it. I am going to give you the inspiration to do it. I will do this so you can go out and do it. You can learn to love people the way I have loved people, and forgive people, and to be selfless with people."

This is God's call. This is where he is walking. He says to us, "I want to give you life. I want to give you this life because I love you."

Stop chasing after your own view of the way the world is supposed to be. Start following the one who made you and who made this world and said to us, "Here are the boundaries. You can do anything you want inside these boundaries, and if you stay inside of them, you will be rich."

It is all about relationships. That is where the good life is. God is leading us to it. Let's follow him.

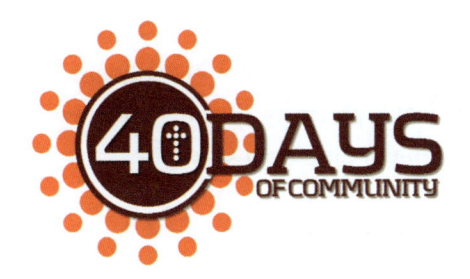

four

Serving Together

... working together with one mind and purpose.
– Philippians 2:2, NLT

Lutheran Church of Hope has become larger than any of us could have dreamed back in 1994 when we began with just a dozen or so members. On most weekends we have between sixty-five hundred and seventy-five hundred worshipers. And at Easter and Christmas, our numbers top sixteen thousand.

At one time we didn't have enough space to accommodate everyone. So today we're thankful to have a sanctuary where we can all fit into one place of worship. No longer do we have people spilling over into the gymnasium and chapel on Sunday mornings.

And while construction and completion of our worship center in 2008 was important, it pales in comparison to building up the kingdom of God. This is why we take seriously the words of Jesus in Matthew 6: "Do not store up for yourselves treasures on earth, where moth and rust destroy and thieves break in and steal." The buildings we occupy are transitory, but the kind of kingdom we are building here at Hope will last for eternity. We are joining with Jesus Christ in building the eternal kingdom of God.

Becoming smaller

One of the ways we build the kingdom of God is to focus on growing smaller even as we become larger as a congregation. Because as strange as this may sound, the more we grow larger, the more we must also grow smaller in important ways.

Let me explain what I mean. The key to building the kingdom of God on earth is to build a sense of community, to draw each of us closer to God and to each other. Today the size of our congregation can be overwhelming, even intimidating to many. This is why we have created hundreds of small groups within Lutheran Church of Hope.

Our goal is for everyone to be part of a small group. There is no way in a church of even one hundred members that people can know each other intimately. There is no way in a church of any size at all that people can experience those around them as brothers and sisters in Christ, to find the closeness of Christian fellowship. This happens only in small groups.

The Bible describes this phenomenon of fellowship through the Greek word *koinonia*, which means being together, getting connected, and living together in community. And by far the best way to experience this *koinonia* relationship is in small groups of three, five, nine, twelve, or perhaps fifteen people.

The small-group experience that has now become so common at Lutheran Church of Hope was developed during the Lenten season some years ago. People showed up in huge numbers to meet in small groups during the week. There was something new and special during that Lenten season as we focused on developing small groups and getting people plugged in.

In the past we had small groups as well, but during that particular Lenten season, each small group had an added purpose. In addition to the staples of fellowship and spiritual growth, all of the groups that year were asked to have a mission dimension. Every small group developed a mission project. There is something special about serving others that transforms our experience together.

Feeding a million—together

As you know by now, the mission we took on during the Lenten season of 2007 was to feed a million people, and the response was spectacular. Halfway through Lent, we had prepared half a million meals. God showed up big time in this event, and the people showed up as well for this mission opportunity. In fact the only complaint we received is that people had trouble scheduling their small groups into the storehouse and finding time to come and prepare the meals to be distributed because so many of the time slots were already filled.

Those who helped prepare the meals during those forty days of Lent learned an important principle: We are much better together. Because together we discovered we could prepare the astonishing number of one million meals, perhaps even more. It was a chance for each of us to live out the gospel message.

One of the goals of *koinonia* fellowship, of meeting in small groups, is that we might find joy. In fact the whole purpose of building the kingdom of God, of building community, is to experience joy. Paul wrote this in his letter to the church at Philippi. Joy should be the center of our life together. Because even while Paul was writing the letter to the church at Philippi from prison, where he faced execution, he nevertheless wrote eloquently and passionately about the centrality of joy.

Paul wrote, "If you have any encouragement from being united with Christ, if any comfort from his life, if any fellowship with the Spirit, if any tenderness and compassion, then make my joy complete by being like-minded, having the same love, being one in spirit and purpose."

Experience true joy

Joy is the key to building God's kingdom, and the way to experience joy is to work together with one mind and purpose. Just think of what we can do together when we respond as a small group. We find our joy complete when we are one in spirit and purpose.

So often, though, we see our spiritual life and growth as a private, personal calling. We believe the Christian life is between just ourselves and God. We spend so much time and energy trying to find God's purpose for us as individuals. And so we find ourselves asking, "What was *I* created for?"

But this is only part of the question. The deeper questions Paul suggests by his letter are: What is God's call for you within community? What is God's call for you to be together with others in the body of Christ? What does it mean to be like-minded, to have the same love for one another? And what does it mean to be one in spirit and purpose? This is God's call to each of us, the call to be in community.

At Lutheran Church of Hope, we already have dozens of missions, dozens of ministries. After all, we are mission-focused just as Jesus was. But we wondered several years ago what could happen if we brought the entire church together around one specific mission. If we were all united in one spirit and purpose, what incredible thing could God do through us?

The vision that came to us centered on the increasing tragedy of hungry, starving people. We have a world filled with plenty, yet millions of people do not even have enough to eat. So we wondered if this one congregation, Lutheran Church of Hope, would come together in spirit and purpose, how many people could we feed? That became the question: *How many people could one congregation feed?* This had probably never been done before quite this way, so we had no clue how many people we could feed.

But we were motivated by that powerful passage in Matthew 25 where Jesus says on the last day we will be judged by how we responded to those who were hungry. We will be judged by how we ministered to those who were thirsty, to those who had no clothes, and to those who were abandoned by this world.

And then Jesus provides some of the most profound, motivating words in all of history when he declares, "Whatever you do, whatever you do for the least of these my sisters or brothers, you do it for me." Whatever you do for the hungry of the world, you do it for Jesus. And this became our vision for Lent that year, to feed a million hungry people because we would be doing it for Jesus.

An impossible challenge

As we were praying about the challenge, we were trying to think as big as we could imagine. We thought that if everything came together just right, if all of us prayed and worked together with one spirit and purpose, perhaps 600,000 or 700,000 meals were remotely possible. Yes, if everything went just perfectly, perhaps we could reach and feed 700,000.

But then in the midst of our prayers, we were moved by the Spirit to say, "Let's shoot for a goal that we cannot *possibly* accomplish on our own. Let's set a goal that could only be attributed to God. Let's do what we have done so often here at Hope—let's see what God can do through us." The result was that we set a goal of preparing and distributing one million meals.

Feeding a Million in Forty Days

The numbers were staggering. But of course, so is the power of our God. Just as Jesus multiplied the loaves and fish and fed the five thousand, so he also multiplied our resources so we could feed a million people.

When we all come together with one mind and purpose, we can accomplish so much more together than individually. There is so much more strength and power and love in community. Not all of us have it together, but together we have it all.

In the case of feeding a million, we were able to build the kingdom of God together. And together we experienced the power and love of God in Jesus Christ. Together we experienced *koinonia*. Together we became united in spirit and in purpose.

By the way, the specific foods we packaged to feed a million people were designed by some of the leading scientists in the world. They found that hungry, starving people cannot absorb much of the foods we normally eat together, so they needed to find something that would be both safe and nutritious. Thus they put together a recipe we followed that was designed specifically to meet the needs of those who are truly starving.

In the process, we found during those Forty Days of Community that we are truly better together. And so today, whenever we do a mission project such as feeding the hungry, we find out how much we need each other. We learn from the Scriptures we are never called to carry out Christ's mission by ourselves.

In fact I would challenge you to find a place in the Bible where God calls us to go out by ourselves and *not* work with anyone else; it just isn't there. We are called to community. We are called to be part of the body of Christ, to work together in building up the kingdom of God.

A team of twelve

Jesus always created community. He had a small group of twelve with him during his entire ministry. When he fed the five thousand with the bread and fish, he sent out his disciples as teams to take the food to the people.

The same is true for Nehemiah. When Nehemiah received a personal call from God to go back from exile in Babylon to the holy city of Jerusalem and rebuild the wall, he didn't do it alone. The book of Nehemiah is all about how we created small groups. Every team had a different function but the same goal.

The goal of rebuilding the wall of Jerusalem, in fact, sounds much like our Mission Riverside. Each weekend during the summer for several years, we had teams that built cottages for Riverside Bible Camp north of Des Moines. Those who had camped there in the past knew how much those new cabins were needed. Over time we completed twelve cottages holding twelve campers each. That's 144 *more* campers each week who can now hear the good news of Jesus Christ. And the cottages can hold campers year-round, for retreats and conferences and adult activities, because they're built that well. And it was all because of teams.

Everything is better in teams, which is why Jesus always worked this way. Paul's missionary journeys were always done with teams. We are always better working together, working in teams, in small groups, building community.

When we serve together, we are united in one spirit and purpose. When we gather together, things are always better. When we join together, we produce far more than we could ever do by ourselves. So just as during the forty days we were called to carry out the vision of working together to feed a million, we are called to work together with one spirit and purpose in all we do.

Living as servants

This is our call as Christians. Jesus never calls us to move closer to the penthouse, spiritually speaking, but rather to move toward the servants' quarters. The deeper we go in our spiritual lives, the more mature we grow as Christians, the closer we come to the servants' quarters.

It is so tempting for us to say today, "Yes, I know, I know. I *know* I should be serving God. But the problem is, I really don't want to serve people. Why can't this just be between God and me? Whenever I try to serve people, it gets so incredibly messy."

Yes, life does get messy. But how can you expect to serve God without serving people? By not serving the crown of God's creation, the women and men created in his image, you miss the whole point of being a servant.

There is really no way to pull the two apart—serving God and serving people. Because if you want to serve God, then you must serve his people. If you are serving people in his name, then you are serving God.

Malachi 3 says it this way: "Bring all the tithes into the storehouse, so there will be enough food in my temple. If you do I will open the windows of heaven for you. I will pour out a blessing so great that you will not have enough room to take it in."

God puts the challenge to us in this passage where he says, "Try it. Put me to the test." This is the only place in the Scriptures where God asks us to put him to a test.

This is the challenge we must respond to. Bring in the offerings of food, God says, and see if I will not open up the heavens and flood you with blessings. Bring in your offerings and I will bless you. This is the only place in the Bible as well that has a conditional blessing so deep. God says, "Put me to the test. Test me out."

Give it away

God says clearly, "Start serving me by serving other people. Most of all, I don't need your packaged food. I don't need your dried vegetables. But you are serving me when you are serving others. You are doing this for *me* when you are helping those who need to eat to survive."

God also says to us, "To whom much is given, much will be required." So if you have been given a lot, a lot of food, a lot of resources, God is saying to us, "I didn't give you all of these blessings just to bless you. I gave you these gifts so that you may share them with someone else."

This is why we brought all the food each week that was needed to feed a million. And this is why we continue giving people the opportunity to give food and money and time, so we can help those who truly need it. God has said, "If I have given you a lot, then I expect you to give a lot. Bring your tithes into the storehouse, so that there will be enough food. If you do this, I will open the windows of heaven for you."

God never gave us an overabundance of food and resources so that we might hoard them. Do you remember what happened to the Israelites in the wilderness when they hoarded the manna rather than sharing it? It all spoiled. Food that is not shared will spoil, and resources that are hoarded grow rancid. We were given much so that everyone in this world might have enough, so that we could serve God by serving other people.

And so in the process we are better together. We are more faithful when we are together. And we are more faithful when we serve together.

Riding the bus

Over spring break our family often goes home to Chicago where my wife and I grew up. And I must admit that I am a Norwegian—I can't help it—which means I am usually frugal. Translated that means "cheap." Sally was hoping we would take cabs around the wide expanse of Chicago, but I bought a five-day bus pass. This is an amazing discovery for visitors. I highly recommend this if you ever go to Chicago. You can take the Chicago Transit Authority bus or the elevated train anywhere in the city. Public transportation will take you anywhere. It is amazing. I wish we had it in Des Moines.

One day we boarded a bus and sat in the only remaining empty seats. And the seats just happened to be right next to the bus driver. We were close enough to develop a personal relationship with the bus driver, whether we wanted to or not, and the driver was having a very bad day.

In fact he was not happy about anything in his world that day. He was especially not happy when people would come up next to him and ring the bell to get off the bus. They seemed to cross some kind of invisible line next to him, because then he would shout, "Get back, *get back*!" People were intimidated by his anger and would apologize, saying, "I'm sorry, I'm sorry." Or some of them would just exacerbate the tension by saying, "Hey, there ain't no line here. I don't see a line!"

And that would cause the driver to explode once again. He would read the riot act of the rules of the CTA and threaten to take away their bus card. At that point I started thinking, "I hope he doesn't take *my* card." The bus driver was mad at cab drivers and others who were sharing the roadways, and he was using colorful adjectives to express his emotions. At one point he literally stuck his head out the window and began shouting obscenities.

He was also greatly angered by people getting on the bus asking how far it would go. "Does this bus go to the blue line train?" they would ask. "Does it go to the Sears Tower?" Finally he just stopped answering questions.

My wife, Sally, had worked in customer service at the Des Moines airport for eight years, and so she started using some of her people gifts on the bus driver. She knew we needed to ask him whether the bus connected with the blue line, and she knew how to do this without provoking him. And of course I did what any macho man would do in a similar situation. I suggested that Sally ask him for directions.

Of course we had been watching the bus driver emote for the past 20 minutes, but I said to Sally, "Would *you* ask him?" Sally has this amazing gift. She can make friends with the angriest person on the face of the earth. So she started making conversation with the driver. "You really have an important job," she told him. "You must know the city of Chicago very well."

The driver started warming up to Sally, although he was still mad at the rest of the world. In fact as they talked, he started getting downright chummy, which I didn't know how to handle. Finally he looked right at me and asked, "Well, what do *you* do?"

I wanted to answer, "Food distribution." But I didn't say that. I answered, "I am a preacher." You could see him processing this answer as we drove down the next couple of blocks. He didn't say anything. Then a cab cut him off and he wanted to explode, but instead he said, "My, my, my." As I was getting off the bus, I noticed he was wearing a big silver cross. And that got me thinking.

We are the message

What are we like out there in the world? For those of us who call ourselves Christians, how do we act out there? Of course Lutheran Church of Hope is for both kinds of people, for those who are Christians and for those who are looking into the faith. But for those of us who call ourselves Christians, we are also wearing the cross.

If people know who we are, then we are also wearing the cross of Jesus Christ. So how do we treat people who cut us off in traffic? How do we treat those who trespass against us? How do we respond to people who cross our lines? How do we respond to those who are considered the least among us? How do we deal with people we would rather ignore?

Our typical response to people we do not deem good enough, to those we would rather ignore, is to keep them out of sight. We tend to avoid them, to send them away whenever possible. When people flocked to Jesus—the sick, children, lepers—the standard response of the disciples was to send them away, to get rid of them. So Jesus had to say rather emphatically to his disciples, "Let them come to me, do not stop them."

Consider the people of Haiti. We didn't really need to feed them, to care about them. It's not our concern that only 20 percent of their land is tillable, which isn't nearly enough to feed their whole population. It shouldn't concern us that they are not getting a fair share of the profits for the coffee they raise because of a lack of leverage in the marketplace.

People starve, right? That's just the way life is. We can so easily dismiss such people by saying, "Hey, it's not in my neighborhood. It is not in our city. It is not our problem. You said we should love our neighbor, but these people are not our neighbors."

But for those of us who are Christians, it is really hard, in fact it is impossible, to ignore Jesus' words in Matthew 25: "Whatever you do, whatever you do for the least of these my sisters and brothers, you do it for me." And Jesus goes on, "I was hungry and you fed me. I was thirsty and you gave me something to drink. I was naked and you clothed me. I was in prison and you visited me. I was sick and you cared for me."

Perhaps you're thinking, "But wait a minute, Jesus. I missed you when you were here. I don't remember seeing you here on earth. I know you lived about two thousand years ago, but I don't remember seeing you in West Des Moines, Iowa. I don't remember hearing that you were in Haiti. I don't remember seeing you on the CTA bus in Chicago. I don't remember seeing you in my office. I don't remember seeing you in the hallways of my school. I don't remember seeing you when I was out with my friends. I don't remember seeing you when I was all by myself. And so I just did whatever I wanted to do. I just did what brought me happiness."

But Jesus says to us, "Whatever you did for them, the people in Haiti, the people in your office, the people in your school, the people you hang out with, you did for me. You did it for *me*."

Here's what struck me as I thought about this: What if Jesus were on my personal bus, my journey of life? And what if I recognized Jesus was on my bus *all* of the time? What if I responded to every person on that bus as if I were responding directly to Jesus? What if I truly believed that whatever I was doing to other people, I was doing to Jesus?

If we could see our lives this way, would it change the way we live? I think it would. I know it would. I believe this is exactly the point Jesus is making in Matthew 25. If you knew it was Jesus who was hungry, wouldn't you feed him? Instead of just saying there are some faceless people in Haiti you don't know, what if Jesus told us it was him we were serving? Then would you be prompted to feed him?

See Jesus in others

Jesus is saying to us, "You have something to give to me. In this case it is food. And you have something else to give to me—a heart full of love." Love is not self-seeking. Love is not selfish, but seeks to serve the needs of others. Remember what Jesus said: "Whatever you do to the least of these, you do it to me.

"If you want to serve me," Jesus says, "you must move into my servant's quarters. If you want to go to the top, spiritually speaking, then you must first go to the bottom. The first shall be last and the last shall be first."

Become the chief servant. Start seeing everybody in your world as people you're called to serve. See them as those God is calling you to love, those whose needs he is calling you to meet. If you have an opportunity to meet the needs of God's people, then meet their needs. And watch what your serving does for them.

And when you serve together, you can do more. When you serve together, it doesn't take as much time. When you serve together, you become more faithful. The Bible says iron sharpens iron, and in the same way, a friend sharpens a friend. If you come together with others in the group, you will have people who will sharpen you, people who will make you better.

Serving together doesn't just mean being more productive or faithful, but it also gets us connected. Colossians 3 describes the Christian life as treating others as we would treat Jesus: "Therefore, as God's chosen people, holy and dearly beloved, clothe yourselves with compassion, kindness, humility, gentleness, and patience." These are the attributes each of us should have.

Consider for a moment the attribute of patience. This is truly a difficult one for many of us. How hard it is for us in this affluent and frenetic culture to slow down, to be patient. Yet the Bible challenges us in Psalm 46, "Be still and know that I am

God." God calls us to *be still*. Patience is essential in our devotional life, and also in our relationships. Because if we are not patient, if we are not still in our relationships, then we will miss some of the best parts.

Speaking of relationships, I have a relationship with the city of Chicago, as I mentioned earlier. But that relationship changes depending on my perspective. When I fly over the city in an airplane, I see the city and relate to it in a certain way. I can see the huge buildings, the lake, the roadways, and the parks.

But when I get off the plane and drive through the center of the city, I perceive it much differently. Now I can see specific buildings. I can see monuments and open spaces and a myriad of vehicles all around me. But when I get out of the car and begin to walk the streets, the city is completely different once again. When I walk downtown, to the river north and the river west and end up around Lincoln Park and Michigan Avenue and then the Magnificent Mile, my experience changes considerably.

When I am walking, I am going to see much more, I am going to notice more. I am going to breathe in the very atmosphere of the city. But when I actually stop walking and become still, I see things that I did not see even when I was walking. There is something about being still that enables us to see the world in a unique way.

Sally and I were walking down Michigan Avenue, and I was at the point that many men get to when they are shopping with their wives. What I was feeling was this sense of, "I just can't go on. I am really having fun with you, dear, but I cannot get myself psyched up to go into one more store."

But she was having a blast. So I said, "You just go in. I will stay right out here. It's a beautiful day (even though it was about to rain) and I am enjoying the scenery. So you go into the store." She was fine with that.

So I waited outside the store. I had nothing to do but wait. I actually stopped and did nothing. Maybe for the first time in years, I just stopped. Outside of my devotional time, it seems as though I rarely, if ever, just stop. I began to think about this experience. I really was out of my element. What do you do when you just stop? Of course, that is the point. You do nothing. "Be still," God says, "and know that I am God."

Learn to stand still

In a sense I was just letting the world come to me instead of searching for it, chasing it. And boy did it come! First a couple came walking up to me and asked, "Will you take our picture?" I answered, "Sure," and got to know them as we talked. It is so very different when you just wait, when you stop doing and are open to whatever comes to you.

Then an Asian couple came up to me, speaking very little English. They were looking for an Office Depot store. For five minutes or so we had a conversation, face to face. I had just been walking the city and I knew exactly where the store was, so I began describing how to get there.

As we were talking, at first it seemed as if they were getting it, and then it seemed as though they were not getting it. We started laughing at our difficulty in communication, and yet we were enjoying the moment. Here we were, three people from very different parts of the world with very different life experiences. But if I hadn't stopped, I wouldn't have had that experience at all.

Then it started to rain. I popped open the umbrella. If you want to imagine a picture, think about this: I am underneath this huge umbrella with two people from China, all bundled together. And while we're huddled together, I'm trying to explain to them how to find Office Depot.

Be more patient, the Scriptures say. This meeting with strangers in Chicago got me thinking: What about those people who are closest to me? What about my family, my best friends? When was the last time I just "stopped"? When was the last time I stopped and asked them, "How are you doing? What is going on in your life?" I had trouble thinking of the last time.

As we drove home from Chicago through Illinois and Iowa, I was sitting in the front seat with our seventeen-year-old son. The other three in our family were in the back seat, playing a game. So my son and I started talking. We hadn't talked like this for a long time, but now we had several hours with nothing to do but talk. I learned about some of his dreams and goals, about the importance of his friends. In the course of our discussion, I learned much about him and he learned much about me.

When is the last time you just stopped? When is the last time you talked deeply with people you love? Make some time. It is what God calls us to be, to be in relationship. It is the relationships you have that will fill you up. So slow down. Stop. Just be. And be still and know that I am God.

Look closely at the people around you. Really look at them, and notice the variety of gifts they represent. Not all of them are wired the same. One is an organizer, a Type A. Others are Type Z who like to have fun, to have a social time. Everyone is unique.

Some of us are joy seekers. And my, how the church needs such people. We would be so boring without them. Others are the relational people who just want to get to know those around them. And then there are the peacemakers, those who keep the whole world going. Whenever they find any kind of conflict, they are seeking to make peace.

How boring it would be if we were all the same. How ineffective we would be. How unproductive it would be, and how less faithful we would be. How much less we would get done.

Imagine how much more connected we could be if we would appreciate people who are different from us. Instead of saying, "If you are not like me, then you are not as valuable as I am," why not appreciate the diversity? Appreciate the variety. We also need to realize that if people were all like us, then the whole thing would fall apart. None of us have it all together, but together we have it all.

And even more important, find the love. Again Colossians 3 says, "And over all these virtues, put on love, which binds them all together in perfect harmony."

While we were in Chicago, we saw the musical *Wicked* that had been playing for several years. The play is about the movie *The Wizard of Oz*. The entire event is a testimony to the talent of the actors, musicians, producers, sound and light technicians, choreographers—right down to the ticket-takers. Everyone has to work in harmony, doing what they have been enlisted to do.

And when it all comes together, when it all happens as planned, it is a highly inspiring event. If you do not get goose bumps in that production, then you had better check your pulse. It is just amazing what we can do together when we are connected, when the human spirit finds extraordinary harmony.

Now multiply that dynamic when we start to do it for God. When we do this for the glory of God, everything multiplies. When I stop and look closely at Lutheran Church of Hope, I am seeing more growth and more beauty each year. It is not growth in numbers I am talking about, but the growth in our love. It is the love for God and the love for one another in the world around us.

This love even became front-page news in Des Moines during Lent when we took on the task of feeding a million people. What made this so attractive is the love for each other and the world. Everyone who was quoted in the article about Hope described preparing all those meals as "a God thing." It *is* a

God thing. It arises from our love for God and for each other and for the world.

That is what gives beauty to a church. When you look at the huge architectural wonder, the sanctuary at Lutheran Church of Hope, you cannot look in the mirror and see just yourself. You have to see all the people around you because it is what we have done together that brings beauty and meaning.

Love binds us together in perfect harmony. It is love that has this incredible power to build the kingdom of God. It is only love that could build this church and connect us to one another.

The power of love

Toward the end of the movie *Little Miss Sunshine*, the plot focuses on the older brother. He is acting out some kind of teenage angst. He has just discovered the devastating news that his lifelong dream of becoming a fighter pilot has been dashed because he is color-blind. In the movie he begins to flip out.

Things are so tense that during one scene he pulls over to the side of the road, runs out of the van and down a steep hill, and collapses in pain and frustration. At that point the teenager wants to completely divorce himself from his family, from anyone. But what he really wants is to flee something else. He is an emotional basket case.

His mother climbs down the hill and tries to console him, to talk him back into the van. But he is not listening. The mother finally returns to her family and says with a sense of helplessness, "I don't know what to do." Finally the father says to the younger daughter, "Olive, little sister, do you think there is something you can do?"

Olive's place in the family is to bring the power of love. After I watched the movie clip for about the fourth time, I saw a sign in the background that read, "United We Stand." We are better together. Don't ever underestimate the power of love.

We get it all messed up in this world. We think power is about winning fights, winning arguments, defeating enemies. But that is not real power. Real power comes through love. The thing that motivates Olive to walk down that hill for her brother is love.

While the mother couldn't reach her son with persuasion, the love of the little sister got through to him. Her love produced a changed heart. Little Miss Sunshine moved the older brother to pick up his little sister and carry her up the hill when she couldn't climb on her own. It was her love that motivated him to apologize and admit he was wrong.

Love is a gift that makes a church most beautiful. The Bible states it this way: "Let your light shine." And the New Living Translation perhaps says it best: "Let your light shine so that your good deeds stand out. Let your good deeds stand out for the whole world to see."

All of this love is so that God, the author of love, might be glorified. It is the power of love that makes us beautiful together. Love makes us more and more beautiful all the time. And that beauty is attractive to the world around us. That beauty is good for the cause of Jesus Christ.

We are much better together when we serve together. We are more productive. We are more faithful. We are more connected. And we are more beautiful.

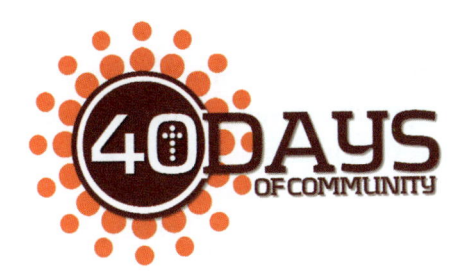

five

Growing Together

Sing praises to God and to his name! Sing loud praises to him who rides the clouds. His name is the Lord— rejoice in his presence! – Psalm 68:4, NLT

Palm Sunday is one of my favorite days of the entire church year. I love Palm Sunday because of the story itself, but also because it launches Holy Week, which is kind of like college basketball's Final Four for us as Christians. Holy Week comprises four important services: Palm Sunday, Maundy Thursday, Good Friday, and Easter Sunday.

We hear a great deal about the national college basketball tournament and the road to the Final Four around the time of Palm Sunday. But I would like to talk to you about a road that is much more significant. It is the road to Jerusalem. It is the road for every one of us, and indeed for the entire world to travel.

It is the road to the cross, and it is about Jesus Christ. And I want to tell you about the invitation God extends to you, an invitation to walk with him on this road. Above all, you need to know this invitation is for you.

Before serving Holy Communion during the worship service, I repeat the words of institution, which a pastor always says. And the words are, "This is the body of Christ, which was broken for you. This is the blood of Christ, which was shed for you."

And then the people come forward and receive the wafer of bread and hear the words, "This is the body of Christ, given for you." And they dip the wafer in the wine or grape juice, and hear the words, "This is the blood of Christ, shed for you."

All of this is for *you*.

Martin Luther, the great reformer of the 16th century who started the Protestant Reformation, said that the words "for you" are the most important words in the Sacrament of Holy Communion. The promise is that the broken body of Jesus is for you. That is the key; it is for you, it is for me, it is for the world, and in believing his blood was shed for you. It was a gift God has given each of us. That is why Holy Week is so pivotal to our faith.

On Palm Sunday, Jesus entered the city gates of Jerusalem, the holy city. He was there on a mission. He was on the way to the cross. On that day he was hailed as king. But by the following Friday, that same crowd would be calling for his crucifixion. Jesus knew they were going to turn on him. It must have broken his heart, but he continued his walk to the cross.

Jesus does this because of his love for you. It was for you that Jesus ascended from the throne. But that throne was a cross. And he put on a crown as well, but it was a crown of thorns.

All of this was for you

Jesus also went to the upper room to show his disciples what he was doing was for them. He washed their feet and gave his disciples the bread and wine because it was for them. And then he went to the cross at Calvary, and it was for them and it was for us. After three days he was raised from the dead, and it was for us.

The Bible says in Romans 6:5, "If we have been united with him in his death, we will certainly also be united with him in his resurrection."

Jesus did not die just so that we could know a story about a religious leader who did these things. He did not die just so we could understand the history, or so we could know what people believed about one who lived and died and rose from the dead. He did this because through faith, we are joined to him.

You belong to Christ

To be a Christian literally means we belong to Jesus Christ. We are one with Christ. Just as he has put to death our sin, he has also put to death our death. Just as Jesus is raised from the dead, we who are united with him are raised to a new life.

Holy Week is a time of walking through the Lenten journey. And what an incredible journey the Lenten season is at Lutheran Church of Hope.

When we determined to help feed a million people during the Lenten season in 2007, we had six hundred people show up one day to help put food packets together. And hundreds more helped many other days during those Forty Days of Community.

I recall that one day we had a crisis while working on this mission. We ran out of the plastic bags we were using to package the food. A woman who lives ninety miles away heard the call, heard about the crisis, and got into her car and drove all the way to West Des Moines so we would have enough plastic bags.

All of this came about as we partnered with Kids Against Hunger, an organization committed to wiping out hunger around the world. The organization feeds between a half million to three-quarters of a million people every three months. As a church, as just one congregation, we were able to push past the one million mark in forty days, just half of that three-month period.

What an awesome thing that was! Somebody told one of our leaders as they were delivering meals in downtown Des Moines, before the meals were shipped to Haiti, "Nobody has been hungry in Des Moines for over a month because of one congregation." And that congregation was Lutheran Church of Hope.

We thank and praise God for such reports. And that wasn't the only story that got back to us. A man walked into my office one Saturday morning during the Lenten season that year and said, "We have been praying about this mission to feed the hungry and heard that we need to send more money to buy supplies and food. We have been led to write this check." And he handed me a check for $20,000. That was a very good Saturday morning, and a very good start. Through such generosity and God's guidance, we were able to reach and surpass our goal of feeding a million people in forty days.

We're able to achieve such efforts when we truly believe the words of Philippians 1:6: "Being confident of this, that he who began a good work in you will carry it on to completion in the day of Jesus Christ." We do believe this, and *did* believe this—that God would complete the mission of feeding a million people through us. It was and is "a God thing," as we're often fond of saying.

God gets the glory

We give God the thanks because our mission of feeding a million was a God thing. It was not our idea—it was *his* idea. God gave the idea to a group of people, and he raised up the leaders. And what an incredible ministry, what an incredible work it turned out to be. It was all so that others could see our good works and glorify our Father in heaven.

People give money to various charities all the time. But for this particular effort of feeding a million, we asked our members to give something much more valuable than money: We needed their time. It is good to give money, of course. And that's easy to do when you have the funds. But when you actually do the work, there's a greater sense of accomplishment and appreciation. And so it was very fulfilling to actually help do the physical work of feeding a million people.

We discovered we had an oversized appetite for helping the people of Haiti, and locally as well. During that effort, our volunteers sent out five hundred to six hundred sack lunches to local shelters every day. They also gave sack lunches to any homeless people they could find. Anyplace they saw a needy person needing a meal, they were reaching out.

And if that wasn't enough, grocery bags bulging with non-perishable foods went to food banks and social service agencies in central Iowa. Fruits, tuna, and chicken—it was a $230,000 relief effort. Thanks to generous individuals, businesses, and corporations, one million starving stomachs were filled.

It was indeed a God thing. And it wasn't to show what we could do, but rather to show what God could do *through* us. Our dream was that those who received the meals would look up and see the food as a gift from God, and they would be blessed. A local TV news anchor reported, "What a great story, what a wonderful thing they are doing out there. It just goes to show what can happen when someone comes up with a great idea."

God working through us

You know, that TV anchorwoman got it right. Because when someone comes up with an idea, and that someone is God, look what happens. Look what happens when the church understands that our work is to set our sails to the wind, the wind of the Holy Spirit. We do not create the wind, but we work with the wind in the direction God is leading. It is not so much doing things for God as letting God do things through us.

When that happens, the Bible says, the imperfect becomes perfect. God's power is made perfect in our weakness. Isn't that ironic? Through our imperfections, God's power is made perfect. It is his love that inspires us to let his Spirit blow through us and do these things. It is his love that empowers us to do miracles in his name.

This is not an overstatement: What we witnessed through the feeding of a million was a miracle. To feed that many people in that short of a time period—well, it just didn't add up. Even the nationwide organization we worked with said it didn't add up. It wasn't humanly possible. It was a miracle!

The generosity and spirit behind that effort, the wind of God's Spirit moving among us, makes sure that God gets the glory. The spirit of love and generosity is attractive to people in this world, which is why so many people showed up to help feed others.

And this is why we gather on Sundays, Saturday night, and during the week as we come together as the body of Christ. We come together to meet the one who has the power. We want to hang out in his house. We don't come to worship services and get in line to receive Holy Communion because we are worthy. We don't come because we deserve anything, or because we are more religious than others in our community. No, we come because God has opened up his house and is saying to us, "Come, I want you to know me better. I want you to walk with me."

A crowd gives praise

Two things intrigue me about Palm Sunday as Jesus entered Jerusalem. For one thing, a crowd showed up. We kind of forget that sometimes. It is so easy to focus on just the palm branches or on the donkey Jesus was riding, the symbol of humility.

It is easy to just focus on the road to the cross. But very rarely do we hear anything about the size of that crowd. We sometimes overlook that Jesus did it for us, and that a spontaneous celebration occurred.

We are told the entire city of Jerusalem was in an uproar about Jesus' entry into the city. "Who is this?" they were asking. "Who is this that brings the people out in such large crowds?" We are told it was a huge crowd that greeted Jesus as he rode into the city. "Who is this Jesus?" people were asking, "Who is he?" Light always attracts people, especially in such a dark world as we live in. Light attracts, and Jesus came as the light. Jesus was the light shining in the darkness.

The second characteristic about the story of Palm Sunday that strikes me is that people were praising God. They were praising God unapologetically, just as we do when we gather each week. When we worship together, we praise God.

We call our time of worship a celebration service. Some call it praise and worship. That is true, and that is why we come together. The Old Testament is full of passages that say again and again, "Praise God." This is who we are. We were created to praise him.

Psalm 68:26 says, "Praise God in the great congregation, praise the Lord in the assembly of Israel." Verse 32 says, "Sing to God, O kingdoms of the earth, sing praise to the Lord, to him who rides the clouds. His name is the Lord, rejoice in his presence."

That kind of language sounds normal, doesn't it? That's because it is so common in the Bible. Over and over we read this kind of exclamation: "Sing praise to God, shout your praises to God, sing to his holy name, rejoice in his presence. His name is the Lord. He alone is worthy."

To be able to celebrate Holy Communion and enjoy fellowship and breakfast at Lutheran Church of Hope—all of this is just a powerful experience of God. All of this is a foretaste of the kingdom of heaven. In Revelation 7, the Scriptures describe a great multitude of people worshiping God. The numbers will be so great that no one can even count them. It is a glimpse of what a portion of heaven will be like.

Part of what we will do in heaven is to worship. It is at the center of our life together, now and forever. But there is another thing we will do in heaven: We are going to serve. We are going to serve God because that is how we will honor him. God has wired us up to serve. It is a need we will always have in our relationship with him.

And we always worship better together. Remember what the book of Ecclesiastes says: "Two are better than one, and three are better than two." I would add, "A thousand are better than three when it comes to worship." There are other times and places where three are better than a thousand, such as in small groups. For the sake of fellowship and discipleship, three are better than a thousand. But worship is always better when we are all together.

People follow the light

Light in the darkness always attracts a crowd. When I was a little kid growing up in Montana, I remember the first time I saw one of those blue searchlights shining up into the sky. You've seen them—those powerful blue lights that shine up into the heavens and weave around in a pattern so everyone can see them.

For an eight-year-old boy, this was about the coolest thing I had ever seen. We were all outside, my brothers and my friends and our neighbors, and we were shouting, "Look at that light!

Look at it. Wow!" We even got someone's parents to drive us closer to the light. And guess where it was coming from? K-Mart, of all places. But that was the idea, wasn't it? The light drew a crowd.

And the light drew the crowd to Jesus on Palm Sunday. It is his light that the world so desperately needs. But Jesus also says to us, "You are the light of the world. Let your light so shine that others will see your good works and praise your Father in heaven." So once again, it's a God thing. It is for his praise, not ours. And it's so important that we understand this. If people start praising you, or start praising a church for what it is doing, make sure you give God the praise because it is *always* a God thing.

I remember back in the early days of Lutheran Church of Hope in the mid 1990s. We were just getting started, and someone had this great idea: What if we had a Saturday evening worship service? What a great idea! The only problem was, hardly anyone else felt that way. So we had some Saturdays when the entire attendance at the worship service was just one person. I was the only person that showed up. I couldn't get my family to come. I couldn't even get the music leader to come.

One person cannot worship, though, so I just turned off the lights and went home. It is the only time in the history of Lutheran Church of Hope that we cancelled weekend services, because you just cannot worship with one. The Bible says in Matthew 18 that wherever two or three are gathered together in Jesus' name, he shows up. But not with just one.

One-on-one time with God is very important, and in fact is essential. But that is not worship. For worship you need someone else. You need someone else around you. And the more that others show up around you, the more powerful worship can become. Worship is another one of those things we do better together. We serve better together, too, and we grow better together. We love people better together. And this is where God's story and our story begin coming together.

God's story becomes your story

Consider your two hands. Imagine that in one hand is God's story, and in the other hand is your story. Sometimes spirituality weaves in and out of both hands and stories. God's story is here in the one hand, and sometimes we feel a little closer to God's story. At other times we think God's story is completely irrelevant to ours, which is the other hand. So God's story and what he has done, at times, seems like it is clear over in the other hand. And when that happens, there are so many things in life that seemingly don't relate at all to God.

So our lives become God's story on the one hand and our story on the other, and quite often they don't seem to merge. But because of the events of Holy Week, this is where God's story and our story become one and the same. This is where our stories become one.

Do you remember all the events preceding Easter? First Jesus rode into Jerusalem through the city gates on a donkey—for you. He went to the upper room to wash his disciples' feet and share his last supper—for you. He went to the cross and died—for you. He humbled himself and suffered a humiliating, painful death for a crime he didn't commit—for you. And he was raised from the dead—for you.

This is where our stories merge, and God does not want us to miss it. He doesn't want us to miss this because it's the whole point of the story. He doesn't want this to be just a series of stories we hear. In fact he does not want that at all. What God wants is for everything to come together in your life and mine.

Join the parade

As stated earlier, my family and I were in Chicago over spring break one year, and we went to the St. Patrick's Day Parade. I don't know what you think of parades, but I generally dislike them. I just do not like parades. They always throw candy into the street and you have to risk life and limb to get it. Then it turns out to be stale taffy you don't want anyway. I can hear people at parades thinking, "Wow, this is so much fun...." But really—what's the point?

Anyway I was standing on the side of the road at the St. Patrick's Day parade in Chicago and it is a little bit cold, a little bit drizzly, and all these people are marching by. They are throwing stuff around, and I am not going after the candy and I am not at all happy to be there.

But then a guy comes by with T-shirts and now I think, "Ooooohhh." And I don't know why. What is it about a T-shirt? As if it would have fit me—who is going to hand out T-shirts that fit a guy my size? That is *not* going to happen. But I still have my hand out for the T-shirt.

And what happens is the guy on my right gets a free T-shirt, and the guy on my left gets a free T-shirt, but I get passed by. No T-shirt for me. Now I am *really* disappointed. I hate parades and I am freezing, and I don't even get a T-shirt. Then the Shriners come by and they start calling out to the person standing right next to me. "Hey Bill, hey, Bill, over here, hi Bill!" I am getting wet and I do not get a T-shirt and nobody is calling out to me.

St. Patrick's Day is such a big party in Chicago. They even turn the river green. Nobody would admit this, but I think they take their mugs and dip them in the water and then advertise for green beer. As the day wears on, fewer and fewer people can tell the difference.

Trust me—this is St. Patrick's Day in Chicago. They keep on marching by. They keep on calling out to Bill standing next to me. He must be a Shriner too. He has access to the performers and I do not. And so as I'm standing there, I'm thinking maybe I should join the Shriners because it seems like the only people having any fun at the parade are my wife and the people who are wired like she is, which is great, and the Shriners and the people who are actually in the parade. And of course, Bill, who is next to me.

The people who are having the best time, though, are the ones that are marching. They are the ones who are smiling. They are the ones jumping up and down, handing out T-shirts. It is a party for all of them. But I just stand there, wet and empty-handed.

Jesus comes to each of us and taps us on the shoulder. He says, "Here comes the Palm Sunday parade. Why don't you join us? Why don't you become one of the marchers?" You may answer, "Well, that's fine for all the religious people around here, for all of those who are in small groups. But I'm not in a small group. And it's great for all of those who participated in the Feed a Million thing, but I am not one of those either. No, I'm here today just to watch, to view the parade. All of this makes sense for them, but it's just not for me."

But Jesus is saying, "It *is* for you. In fact it's you I want the most. Because I want to show you things you have never seen. I want you to experience life and joy you cannot experience unless you walk with me. I want you to become a participant, not just an observer. I want you to *do* Christianity, not just look at it."

'I want *you* to drive!'

When I was fifteen years old I got my driver's permit. We lived in Chicago at that time, and my parents had flown to the Twin Cities. My dad was speaking at some church event—he was a pastor. I cannot remember why, but my two brothers and I—one older and one younger—had to stay home for a couple of days. But then my brothers and I were going to drive together to meet my parents in the Twin Cities.

This was about an eight-hour drive from Chicago to the Twin Cities back when the speed limit was just fifty-five miles per hour. That dates me a lot, doesn't it? My brother was eighteen and a senior in high school, so he could legally drive. He could handle it. As for me, though, I had never driven on a freeway.

Just as we pulled outside the suburbs of Chicago, my brother Dave pulls the car over to the side of the road and says to me, "Here, Mike, *you* drive." I was really pumped when he turned the keys over to me. I asked him, "How long do you want me to drive? Perhaps to Rockford?" Rockford was about an hour away.

"No," he said, "drive all the way to Highway 494 in the Twin Cities, which will be about seven hours. When you see 494, wake me up because I am really tired. I'm going in the back seat." Looking back now, I think this was highly illegal. But he said, "I'm going to be in the back seat, and you wake me up when you get there."

I am just loving this—absolutely loving it. (My mother told me many years later she never knew about all this.) But now I am driving the car, my big brother is sleeping in the back seat, and I am loving this!

My little brother, though, is sitting next to me up front, riding shotgun, and is freaking out, keeping up a constant litany: "Watch out for that truck!" "What are you doing?!" "You're going too fast!" He had the Rand McNally road atlas opened up all the way, looking at every marker.

Understand that when I got in that car, I had no expectation whatsoever that I would be driving. I thought I would be bored to tears, looking out the window at nothing but cows and more cows. I thought that was going to be my whole experience, one more time. But when I got the keys, everything changed. That was one of the most exhilarating experiences of my entire life up until that point.

Do you see what I am getting at? You might be thinking, "This is all too new to me, and I have only the equivalent of a religious driving permit. I don't know the Bible all that well. And I've never done any of the stuff you always talk about." But the word to you from Jesus is simply this: "Come follow me. *You* drive. I don't want you to watch, I want you to drive. So just come and follow me. Just come with me now. Come and follow me."

The Forty Days of Community when we fed a million people in 2007 was not just a program. It was not just an event or a one-time exercise to see what we could accomplish. No, that mission was meant to bring a lifestyle change. We didn't want it to be like a fad diet. We wanted it to take root. We wanted it to become our story. We wanted it to become part of who we were rather than just something we did.

What was important was the momentum, the movement, the direction, and the passion that came forth as we labored together to feed a million. It was the fact that we were *doing* Christianity. Because being a Christian is not just something we talk about, but something we do. What we started during Lent that year is something we should never stop doing.

Christianity is something we do. So if you are in a small group, make sure your group is moving. And if you're not in a small group, join one. Find a group where you fit in. Don't just settle in and become self-centered. Keep moving, keep going. Keep doing those things that will produce joy in your life. There are all kinds of ways to get involved. The point is that you're moving. Keep marching in the parade.

For those of us at Lutheran Church of Hope, the experience of feeding a million prompted a lifestyle change among us. This is now who we are, and this is who God is calling us to be. As a result we have learned to love each other better and we have learned to love the world around us better. In worship we have learned to love God better. And so we are better together in whatever we do.

The point for all of us is to keep moving and keep it going. Find where you fit in. Opportunities are all around. Volunteer to work with the youth, or volunteer for a mission trip overseas. Volunteer for *something*.

You can volunteer within your congregation. At Hope we even have a group that volunteered to "foof up" the women's restrooms. I love that idea. I have no idea what "foofing up" the restrooms means, nor will I ever be blessed by it. But I think it is a great idea. Another small group at Hope decided they would start feeding the parking lot attendants on Sunday mornings. Isn't that awesome?

If not now, when?

If you're not involved with a small group of people working toward a common cause, you're not connected. What are you waiting for? What are you going to do with the rest of your life?

As a pastor, it is clear to me that life is fragile and very short. Perhaps it is because I am around death more than most people. Hospitals and funerals are often a part of my day. So again I ask, what are you waiting for? When are you going to get going with your life? I say this with love and as someone who does not always get it right, so don't misunderstand me. But if not today, if not here and now, when are we going to become the church God calls us to be?

Forty Days of Community in 2007 was a great experience. But now we need to keep it going. And do you know what it will take for it to continue? Surrender. That's the key—total surrender of your life. This is the most surprising part of the journey for people, and is also the point where most people stop driving. Because Jesus comes right alongside us and says, "You know how I asked you to join the parade? I want you to come with me and follow me, all the way to the cross. Follow me to the empty tomb, and I will show you that it is for you."

Jesus literally gave his body and blood for you. He didn't come just to tack on some spirituality in your life. He didn't die just so you could become prosperous or comfortable. In fact, that wasn't his point at all. He died so he could teach all of us how to love.

On the other hand, he didn't die so that you could read a book titled *The Secret* and tap into some kind of mystery inside of you. He didn't die so that you could become rich and famous. That is not what spirituality is all about. Christianity is never a self-centered pursuit, but is always a Christ-centered pursuit.

And we start by doing the same things Jesus did. We give up our lives—that's what is meant by surrender. We give up the pursuit of our own happiness and chase after God's happiness instead. We realize what we were created to be and to do.

So what are you going to do with the rest of your life? If you want to be fulfilled and satisfied as a person, you need to pursue God instead of your own self-centered dreams. It is so easy to say, "Well, thanks for the grace and the blessing, but I am not going to go that far. It doesn't look that attractive to me."

Give up control

In order to surrender your life to Christ, you are going to have to let go of the steering wheel. You are going to have to let go of control of your life. It is so easy for us to say, "I may not always make the best decisions, but I like to be in control. I am not going to let anyone else take control of my life, that is for sure."

But I am not asking you to let another human being take control of your life. That would be unhealthy and enabling. I am asking you to let your Creator take control of your life. You can trust him. He is the one who wants to give you the most abundant life of all. He is the one who wants to fill you up.

But he can't do this if you are holding on so hard to the steering wheel. It is easy for us to say, "God, I just want you to sit beside me in the front seat, to be my copilot. I want to drive." But God says, "If you will let me drive, if you will trust me and turn your life over to me, I will show you colors you never knew existed. I will show you things you never imagined were possible. And I will show you what you were really created to be and do. I will show you how to be a lover of people. I will show you how to love me and to love others."

That is where the good life is found, but you have to let go to get there. You have to let go of the steering wheel and let God drive. Who is driving your life? Who is in control? Could you or anyone else do a better job of running your life than the one who created you?

As a matter of fact, we are never going to make the right decisions on our own. The way we always seem to do it is to make decisions based on what we want, and then we try and talk God into them. That is very different from asking God what he wants for our lives. It is very different from saying, "Lord, I trust you."

I hope you can say in your heart, "You are my Lord, and I trust you. Jesus, take the wheel. Jesus, take my life." When that happens, everything around you changes. The New Testament is full of passages that describe this new life. This is the big theme of the Scriptures, the sanctified life.

Galatians 2:20 is just one of dozens of verses that point to this theme: "I have been crucified with Christ, and I no longer live, but Christ lives in me." And here is the deal: If you just watch Jesus in the parade on Palm Sunday, and you just observe Jesus on the cross, you are on the sidelines. You don't really know that he died for you because you didn't go with him. You didn't let his story become your story. Rather it is just a fact you ponder, and you may wonder whether it really happened at all.

But if you will go with him, you will see that his death was for you. You will *experience* that it was for you. And you will be filled with a new life. Your old self will be put to death, you will be crucified with Christ, and it will no longer be you who lives but Christ who lives in you.

You will no longer be doing spirituality for God, but God will be doing it through you. There is such a huge difference between these two stances. And this is the same question that challenges the church: Are we going to be a church that does ministry and carries out programs for God, or are we going to be a church that surrenders to God? Are we going to be a church that lets go of the steering wheel?

Can we honestly ask the question, "Lord, what do you want to do next with Lutheran Church of Hope?" As imperfect yet willing servants, we need to be able to say to God, "You be the Lord, you drive. We love the view. We would not have been a part of the feeding a million people if it were not for you, if we had not let go of the wheel, if it had not been a God thing."

If the forty days of Lent in 2007 had been just an activity of Lutheran Church of Hope, we might have fed 80,000 or perhaps 150,000 people. When you let go of the wheel, however, it becomes a million. It becomes 1.2 million or 1.4 million, or maybe even more.

In addition, a major lifestyle change occurred in us during those forty days because we chose to let go of the wheel. For those of us at Hope, it caused us to ask whether we truly got in the habit of giving to others out of love or whether it was just another program. In the same way, each of us must ask whether we are truly running with Jesus or merely watching him go by in the parade.

Let your light shine today

Imagine your life is a football game, and right now is halftime. Or perhaps it's the third quarter. Each of us has from a few days to several decades remaining in our lives. That is not a lot of time. Life is fragile, and it goes by quickly. The Bible compares our lives to the blink of an eye. That's how short life really is.

You've probably heard someone say that "the days just seem to fly by." The older we get, the faster life seems to go by. Those who are in their sixties and seventies can readily attest to this and have so much to teach the rest of us. Life goes by so quickly.

The Bible says God's power is made perfect in weakness. It is not that we are perfect, but rather that he takes our love and makes the imperfect perfect. In 1 Corinthians, Paul writes that the imperfect becomes perfect when we let God get ahold of us. God can do that with our love. It is God's love for us that inspires us to share our love with the world around us so others can hear the words of Christ's promise.

So what are you waiting for? Whatever time you have left on this earth, love people and love the world around you. Shine light into darkness. There will be no darkness to shine your light upon in heaven. This is it—today is the day of salvation because today is all we have. This is the only opportunity we have to shine the light into darkness. And as you allow your light to shine in the darkness, remember that God is sending us out together. This is not a game; this is real life. God is sending us out to be the light of the world. God is sending us out to love people. He is sending you to love them.

six

Living & Loving
Together

For sin is the sting that results in death ... But thank God! He gives us victory over sin and death through our Lord Jesus Christ. – 1 Corinthians 15:56–57, NLT

Do you believe in miracles? During the Lenten season of 2007 we accepted a challenge that we knew was impossible—to feed a million people in forty days. We knew from the beginning we could never meet this challenge without the awesome power of God. We knew this goal was so far beyond our own abilities that it would take a miracle to accomplish it. We knew none of us could do it alone, but we believed that together, with the power and grace of God in Jesus Christ, we had a shot at achieving the goal.

Our first priority was for everyone at Lutheran Church of Hope to join a small group. We all needed to be part of a team because we believe we are better together, and in fact we're much better together than as individuals. So the formation of small groups became our goal during that Lenten season. And guess what happened? Thousands responded. Small groups sprang up everywhere.

People were no longer just part of a church, of a large congregation, but became part of a community. Eight to twelve people came together to love each other, pray for each other, and serve each other through small groups. There is something potentially transforming about being in a small group, and the overwhelming majority of people at Hope are now in some sort of small group because of that emphasis during the Lenten season in 2007.

Along with getting people involved through small groups, the second challenge was to feed the hungry. The small groups were created not only to experience fellowship and friendship, but also that they might have a specific mission focus. Every small group was invited to be involved in a mission, and the mission was to feed the hungry.

The response was very simply an incredible miracle. More than 1.5 million meals were prepared and sent to Haiti, which is the poorest nation in our hemisphere. Thousands of pounds of food also flowed into Hope to be shared with hungry people in Des Moines. By working together, in just forty days we were able to achieve far beyond what any of us could have imagined.

And while feeding a million people was indeed a miracle, the greatest miracle that ever happened is someone dying and rising from the dead. The miracle is about someone who destroyed the power of death so that you and I could live forever. And that person is Jesus Christ.

Two important questions

Regarding this miracle of Jesus' resurrection, there are two important questions for you to consider. The first question is this: Do you believe Jesus is who the Bible says he is? That is, do you trust the Bible? Do you believe the Bible is telling the truth about Jesus? And so this is the truly critical question: Do you believe the Bible is telling the truth?

Even many well-known theologians today say they do not believe the Bible is telling the truth about Jesus. They cherry-pick certain parts of the Bible to support their own suppositions, then dismiss the rest. Theologians aside, our benchmark question is: Do *we* believe Jesus is who the Bible says he is?

The first question tends to be intellectual in nature while the second question is more personal. And the second question is this: Do *you* believe the Bible? Does your mind affirm that what the Bible says about Jesus is true? Here's another way of stating the question: Do you have a personal relationship with this Jesus who is revealed in the Bible? Do you know him? Do you know about him, or do you really know him?

Of course you might reply, "How can I have a personal relationship with someone who is dead?" Certainly you can accept the fact that Jesus was a man who lived two thousand years ago. You can readily accept that he lived in the Middle East and walked around in what is now called The Holy Land. You can even accept that he was crucified on a cross. But the much tougher question is how you can have a relationship with Jesus, especially if he is dead.

This seems to be the stumbling point for so many people today. How can we be in relationship with someone who is dead? How can we be up front and personal with someone who is not here, who is not present? And this is the question that stymies so many scholars and historians. Jesus died, and we cannot have a relationship with someone who is dead. And of course if Jesus is dead, then there are no miracles. If Jesus is dead, then there is no transformation, no new life, and no salvation.

This is why we need Easter. How desperately we need Easter today. Easter brings us the absolutely stunning news that Jesus Christ is not dead at all, but rather is very much alive. Do you recognize the significance of this? Do you sense it in the very center of your being? Jesus is not dead, but is alive. And because Jesus is alive, this brings us hope. It brings us undying, surprising, magnificent hope!

Perhaps the most familiar Bible passage of all, John 3:16, says, "For God so loved the world that he gave his only begotten Son, that whosoever believes in him should not perish but have everlasting life." Jesus loved us so much that he went to a cross and put our sins to death. But that is not the end of the story. Good Friday is not the final stanza. Easter tells us that not even death could contain him. Not even death could destroy him.

Three days later Jesus was raised from the dead. The stone was rolled away. And this is the incredible news, that Jesus is alive. He is alive! And because he is alive, this is a Jesus you can actually get to know. Jesus is God whom you can get to know. All of this is possible because he has risen. You can get to know Jesus because he is alive. And because Jesus is alive, you can also be alive, truly alive, now and forevermore.

What amazing news. This living Christ, this Son of God, now wants to have a relationship with us. This is not some God who created the earth and then went off to do other things. This is a living Christ who wants to know us and be known by us. This is where our hope comes from. Jesus wants to live with us and in us, to be in relationship with us.

What a mess we've made

When we look around at the world today, we can all see that it is such a mess. We see that the world is filled with despair, hopelessness, and incessant hatred and violence. We see death all around us. Life often does not unfold the way we want it to. But in spite of all of our disappointments and failings, Jesus is alive and he gives us this powerful message of hope.

Easter is about miracles. Easter is about the greatest miracle of all: Jesus has risen from the dead. Jesus is alive, and he gives us life eternal.

The Easter message tells us that God looked squarely into the face of the greatest enemies in this world, sin and death, and has already won the ultimate victory. God has won the victory over sin, death, and the power of evil. God did this for you and for all of us. This is the miracle, that because Jesus has overcome the power of sin and death, we also can live.

One of the surpassing truths about God is that he is absolutely real and genuine. There is no pretending with God, no sleight of hand regarding who he says he is. Scripture tells us that Jesus Christ is the same yesterday, today, and forever. He is always consistent and real. And the challenge he is making today is that we follow in his path, that we also become honest and consistent and real.

And you know this is incredibly difficult for us. We are so often anything but real and honest. We so often live our lives in pretense, pretending to be something we are not. We have this mask we put on to keep others from seeing us as we really are. But one of the purposes of Easter is to bring about a miracle, a miracle of helping each of us become who we really are. It is meant to help us become real with one another.

Why so much suffering?

Our lives always seem to be rooted in ambiguity. On the one hand, we were overjoyed by the response at Lutheran Church of Hope during the Forty Days of Community in 2007, the response to the needs of the poor and hungry. The miracle of feeding a million people far exceeded what any of us could have done alone or apart from God's leading and direction. But on the other hand, that accomplishment also made us much more aware of how deep and broad are the sufferings in the world. We recognize that even after helping feed a million people, we hardly made a dent.

Our world continues to be filled with so much heartache and darkness. Suffering, disease, terror, and war seem to be overwhelming our entire planet. We also see in our own lives and relationships that death is never far from us. Many of us have experienced deep sorrow and loss in recent months.

Many of us are desperately searching for hope. We would love for all the heartache of life to just go away. But we know this is not going to happen on this side of eternity. Life is never going to be perfect, and it is never going to be all sunshine and roses. Instead we are challenged to admit that we live as frightened, helpless, lost human beings. No matter how strong we think we are, just underneath the surface we know how vulnerable, empty, and fragile we really are.

The only way God can get through to us is if we become completely honest. This is not a common response for most of us. We are much better at pretending than we are at being truly real. But just going through the motions and putting on a happy face is not going to cut it.

The underlying reality of the world today is pain, heartache, suffering, and death. And if we are honest with ourselves, we would all confess that we have a broken heart. Life has not worked out quite the way we had hoped. And we don't seem to be able to do much to change it.

Freedom from pretending

God gives us the permission and freedom to stop pretending. The good news is that we don't have to try to be something we are not. We do not have to pretend that we are God, that we are invincible. Rather, God comes right into our lives the way we are, right where we live. God loves us today just as we are, warts and all. God comes to us at the moment of our greatest need and helps us become real.

It is so easy in our culture, and even within the confines of the church, to pretend that we are something we are not. We would like to exude the attitude that we have it all together, that life is a bowl of cherries. It is so easy to pretend we are superhuman, that we do not struggle with the seven deadly sins of pride, envy, greed, lust, laziness, waste, and anger. It is so easy to delude ourselves into believing that temptation does not really affect us even though it happened to Jesus.

But the reality of life, of our individual lives, is that sin stings each of us. Reality is that our sin leads to death. Writing in Romans 7, Paul describes our situation this way: "I am all too human. I am a slave to sin. I do not understand my own actions. For I do not do what I want, but I do the very things I hate." These are words of discernment: I do not do what I want to do, but I do the very thing that I hate. Paul says that he cannot even make the right choices between good and evil.

What are we pretending to be today? Are we pretending to be more spiritual than we really are? How tempting that is today, especially for those of us in the church. Or perhaps we are pretending that we are among the chosen few who truly deserve God's love and favor. Perhaps we pray with the pharisee, "God, I thank you that I am not like other people."

But remember that grace is God's unearned love and favor. The reason that grace is so amazing is that it is free. It is truly a gift from God. Why then are we so fixated on pretending that we somehow deserve God's favor and are not like other folks? Because if grace comes only to those who deserve it, then it is no longer grace.

As church people we are in the greatest danger of pretending we can stand proudly before God and talk about our good works, our spirituality, our morality, and our integrity. But whenever we become honest before God, we instead must admit that our lives are just as messy as those of anyone else. We must admit that none of us can escape the clutches of sin. We are all slaves to sin, the Scriptures say, and sin weighs us down.

Do you sense today that you are weighed down with sin? Is it a heavy burden you are carrying? Sin weighs us down and locks us up. Worst of all, sin deceives us. Sin often makes us think we are something that we are not. The Bible says, "If we say we have no sin, we deceive ourselves." If we fall into the trap of pretending our lives are not a mess, that we can manage to avoid the darkness and dirt of life all by ourselves, then we have deceived ourselves and the truth is not in us.

This is why Jesus died on the cross for us and rose from the dead. Easter helps us admit that we are sinners. It helps us see we have fallen short of the glory of God. Easter helps us admit that we are powerless over sin, death, and the power of evil. Easter helps us realize that we need a Savior.

1 John 1:9 gives us the answer to our predicament: "If we confess our sins, he who is faithful and just will forgive our sins and cleanse us from all unrighteousness." When we confess our sins, Jesus will cleanse us and make us whole. This is the miracle of Easter. We have created a mess of our lives, and then we try to cover it up. But Easter announces that Jesus has defeated the mess and given us new life.

* * *

Some years ago my wife and I decided we needed a larger home for our growing family. That meant we needed to sell our home, which had originally been the parsonage but which we had purchased from the church. We found a new house that we liked, which wasn't all that much larger than our present home, but it was configured differently and seemed to be a better fit for our growing family.

We were just about to put our house on the market when word got around the church that we were planning to sell our house. A couple of families showed interest in looking at our home and perhaps buying it. We invited them to stop over and see the house at their convenience.

One evening when Sally was out and I was home with the kids, I received a phone call from one of these families. They were going to be in the neighborhood and wondered whether they could stop by to look at our house.

To put it mildly, the house was a mess. More than a mess, it was a disaster. No one reading this could probably identify with the situation, because I'm certain that everyone else's home is always perfectly clean and picked up all the time. But that was not the case with our house, and especially not with teenage boys in the house.

My own view is that there is super-duper clean and then there is acceptable clean. Super-duper clean is what you do before company comes over, but rarely lasts very long. Acceptable clean means that if someone stops over unannounced, the main room is clean and you will not take them on a tour of the rest of the house.

And then there is what I call embarrassingly messy. You know what I am talking about. Whenever the house is in the state of embarrassingly messy, you would be mortified if someone were to just stop by unannounced. So into that situation of embarrassingly messy the phone call came: "Ten minutes, can we stop by?"

I hung up the phone, panic-stricken. I have never moved faster in my life. I did not want anyone to see our mess, so I was running all over the house. I was cleaning certain rooms, shoving some of the mess into closets. I pushed a bunch of stuff into the storeroom, telling myself that these visitors would never dare to go into that room. I would tell them that we have such a room, but then I will physically stand in front of the door and not let them in.

I was picking up stuff with my arms, legs, and feet, and I was cleaning as fast as I could go. Finally, just as I squeezed the last bit of stuff into the front closet, the doorbell rang. I opened the door, sweating profusely. The guests asked me, "Have you been working out?"

For the next half hour I showed them the house. I never did stop sweating. Maybe it was just because I was nervous that they would look in one of the closets. It is so easy to pretend in life that we do not have any messes, or to just hide them away in a closet somewhere. I am sure that the people looking at the house knew I was hiding the mess. They knew and I knew that they knew.

Cleaning up our messes

On a more serious and personal level, God knows all about our messes. God sees our personal mess, and there is no way we can just push it into a closet. God knows when we get angry and when we do not use the gifts he has given us. God knows when lust leads to adultery, or fuels a pornographic addiction. Depending on which study you read, one out of four, or perhaps as many as one out of two Christian men struggle with pornography.

The temptation is to try and sweep all of this away. We try to ignore the messes in our lives. We pretend that adultery is not an issue. We pretend that laziness is not an issue, and that greed is not an issue. It is so easy to say to ourselves, "I am not greedy. I am not envious of someone who has a bigger house or a newer car or nicer clothes. I am not envious if someone can afford better vacations. That is not a problem for me."

You see, if you were to ask me, I don't have a problem. I don't have any messes in my life. But God wants to show us that we need to come clean. We need to be honest with God and with ourselves. God says to us today, "I know where you live. I know what you are doing. I know you are tempted to hate when I call you to love. I know you are tempted to judge people by the color of their skin, their ethnic background, or their economic status. I know what is in your heart, for that is the condition of sin."

Let's not be a church that pretends. Let's not be a church that pretends we do not face the darkness. Let's be a church that admits we are sinful and unclean. Let's admit the mess we have made of our lives. Let's admit that we have issues—pride issues, hate issues, greed issues—and they are killing us. That's the heart of the problem, isn't it? Our sin is killing us. If we get real with God, then he can get real with us.

Martin Luther was asked one day what sins we should confess. He responded, "The ones that are bothering you." Can you name the sins that are bothering you? Can you be this honest with yourself and with God? Jesus says he wants you to be free. And in order to be free, you have to know the truth and tell the truth. The truth is what sets you free. In John 8 Jesus says, "If you hold to my teaching, you are really my disciples. Then you will know the truth, and the truth will set you free."

But in order to know the truth, you must be honest with God. You may have never done this before. But today, right now as you are reading these words, be totally honest with God. Let this be the day your transformation occurs. Let this be the day you are no longer just going through religious motions.

If you are wondering how to do this, how to be totally honest with God, Jesus told a powerful parable in Luke 18 that shows how we should pray. Two men went up to the temple to pray. One was a pharisee, a religious leader, and the other was a tax collector. The pharisee proclaimed loudly, "Lord, I am here to remind you of how good a person I am. Remember, Lord, I am a very religious person. I do religious things. I pray all the time. I fast and I tithe. I am truly one of the most faithful people around."

It is so easy for us to sound like this pharisee: "Lord, I do so many religious things. I am one of those who truly deserve your love and favor. I am here to remind you that I am one of the good people of this world. I am one of your best people."

Or are we like the second man Jesus describes? The tax collector was truly a shameful charlatan in those days. He lived a really messy life. He stole from the poor and lined his own pockets with their hard-earned money. But this day the tax collector comes into the temple and kneels down and prays very quietly a simple prayer: "Lord, be merciful to me, a sinner."

Perhaps for the first time in his life, the tax collector is coming clean: "God, I am telling you the truth. I am so tired of not being free. I am so tired of living in bondage. I am so tired of faking it. I am so tired of walking that road to nowhere. I want to be free, truly free!"

Would you like to be truly free? Perhaps inside you are thinking, "Lord, I want to experience a new life today. I want this to happen to me. I want to know that you can raise me up as you did your son, Jesus, and that you can deliver me from death as you did for him. I want to know that you can deliver me from this sin that weighs me down. I want above all to be honest today, because I believe that when I live in the truth, you will set me free. Lord, I confess that I am a sinner. Have mercy on me. I am not here to pretend I am something I am not. I have sinned, Lord, and fallen short of your glory."

Which of these two men that Jesus describes, the pharisee or the tax collector, do you resemble? Remember that Jesus asks, "Which of these two men went away justified?" We need to bring our messes to God, and we need to be honest. Remember that our messes do not hurt God nearly as much as they hurt us.

Our greatest problem

What do you think is our greatest problem in the world today? Some say our greatest problem is terrorism. Others say it is war or violence, or the breakdown of the family. But I would say that if you look closely, our greatest problem is sin. Sin is the root cause of all of our problems. Sin is at the root of all of our broken relationships and our shattered dreams. The real issue is sin.

We so often look at the world and wonder why it has become so messy. We look around and cry out, "God, why did you let all of this happen? Why do you allow so many tragedies? Look at the mess we are making of this world. Why do you allow this, God? Why don't you just fix everything? Why don't you put a stop to war? Why don't you just end all the suffering? Why don't you cure all the diseases?"

You might be thinking, "But wait a minute. Are you saying I got a disease because I am a sinner?" No, I am not saying that. Sometimes bad things happen to us because we cause them. Sometimes someone else sins against us, and that causes us pain or heartache. Sometimes, though, and this is the hardest to accept, we get sick or suffer heartache or face the reality of death for reasons completely unknown.

But this is the world we live in. We're not yet in heaven. Ever since the Garden of Eden, ever since The Fall, there has never been any promise from God that life would be perfect. This is why people always get tripped up on the issue of suffering in life. We arrogantly demand to know why God allows certain things to happen in life, as though God owes us an answer.

He hears our cries, feels our pain

One thing we need to hear today is that God understands our cries, our heartache, and our pain. He even gave us the language to use, the script. Consider Psalm 22, where the psalmist writes, "My God, my God, why have you forsaken me?" These are the words Jesus used on the cross. Sometimes we shout them out as well. "God, how come I am sick? How come my friend is sick? How come my loved one died?" In this world we are so often crying and facing death. We are lost and desperate.

Put yourself in the story of Mary Magdalene. She came to the tomb of Jesus early on Easter morning. She was hurting in the core of her being. She was one of Jesus' closest followers, and called him teacher. There was this incredible bond between them. Sometimes teachers are a gift from God and help turn our lives around, and that is what Jesus was to Mary. When Jesus died on the cross, Mary was there. Eleven of the twelve disciples had fled, but Mary was there.

And on Easter morning, the day after the Sabbath and the first opportunity they had to visit the tomb, Mary came with some other women to the tomb. According to their religious custom, they had come to anoint Jesus' body. But when the women arrived, they realized the tomb was empty. The stone had been rolled away.

Mary immediately ran back to get Peter and John, and they ran with her to the empty tomb. Peter also really needed to be there at that moment. He needed to see the empty tomb because he was carrying a mountain of guilt. Peter had bragged so emphatically, "I will never deny Jesus, I will never abandon him." But then a few hours later, Peter shouted out, "I never knew the man. I was never a disciple."

Peter was lost. Mary was also lost, but for a different reason. She was lost because she was so broken. She was crying out, "Why, God, do good people have to die?" That is also often our cry: Why do good people have to die, and why do the people we love have to die?

As a pastor I have the privilege—and it is a huge privilege—of sitting with grieving families. I have the privilege of being with families when they are experiencing death and planning a funeral. I always want to be there to listen to them, to share in their grief, and to hear their stories about the one who has died.

I recall one incident where a family member had just died—yet another death that seemed to have occurred long before it needed to happen. The brother of the man who had died was sitting there with us, and for almost an hour he did not say more than two words.

But finally he could remain silent no longer and said, "My younger brother was always my hero. I am so broken up today." A little later the wife of the man who had died said, "We had a wonderful life together. It was the best time of my life." Death hurts so bad that it stings.

The week after Easter some years ago, I came home after Sunday worship services and got a call from my younger brother. "Mike, I don't know how to tell you this, but dad just died," my brother told me. "He died suddenly, just dropped over dead." And right away came my response, much like Mary Magdalene must have felt: "God, where are you? This was my teacher. This was the man who changed my life!"

This is what I miss so much about my dad. I am sure he is here today, but I am sure the parties in heaven are so much better than here. I don't think he really wants to be here today, and he knows that I am coming to be with him very soon. Today I am OK, but it still hurts.

What a mess of a world we live in. And right in the middle of the mess, Jesus shows up. This is the good news today. No matter what our messy lives might entail, Jesus shows up in the midst of death, in the midst of grief, in the midst of pain.

Jesus showed up for Darrell, who was from a very poor family in Hudson, Iowa. This was the first funeral I ever had to lead. I went out to Darrell's house when I heard that his son, age forty-two, had just died from a heart attack. It was a shock, completely unexpected. This was a son who had lived in his parents' home all of his life as they farmed together. I sat down with the family and offered to read some Scripture.

I chose the powerful words from John 11, "I am the resurrection and the life. Anyone who believes in me will live, even after dying." After I read the passage, Darrell looked me in the eye and said, "Read it again." Several more times, Darrell said to me, "Read it again."

God shows up right in the midst of our pain and sorrow, even in the midst of death. God doesn't show up just in the glorious times, but he shows up right in the midst of the wasteland, right in the midst of the mess.

And he says to us, "You come to me. You come to me, all who are weary and heavy burdened, and I will give you rest. You come to me, for my yoke is easy and my burden is light. You come to me and I will give you rest for your souls. You come to me, you who are lost. You come to me, you who are desperate. You come to me, you who are in grief. You come to me, those of you who for the first time in many years have come clean. You come to me, you who have confessed your sin. Come to me."

Jesus is calling to each of us. And we can come clean before him and respond, "Come to me, Jesus. I am lost without you. I am desperate for you." God shows up right in the middle of the real world we're living in today. He says to us, "I am not trying to avoid your messes. I am not saying I will come to you only when you make it to a spiritual mountaintop. I will come and find you in the midst of your mess. I will come and be with you in the midst of your sin. I will come and find you in the midst of your grief. I have your sin covered. I have your death covered."

1 Corinthians 15 says, "The sting of death is sin. But thanks be to God who gives us the victory through our Lord Jesus Christ." I cannot stop sinning. I am not going to be able to keep myself from dying some day. But thanks be to God, he has won a victory over sin and death through our Lord Jesus Christ. This is like a fountain, like a spring of water that bubbles up in my soul. The Bible says that those who drink the water God gives them will never be thirsty again. This is what Jesus says to us. It becomes a fresh bubbling spring within us, giving us eternal life.

We are not talking about new life just to help you get through the day. We are talking about eternal life. This is forever. Eternal life is the greatest gift of all. It puts all of our suffering into perspective. It puts our pain, our sin, and our human condition into an eternal perspective. It gives us hope and reminds us of who we are and what we are destined to become.

The best is still ahead

The life we have this side of heaven is just the blinking of an eye—a fleeting moment relative to eternity. This is not to say that your life is insignificant, however. Jesus broke into this life to show us how important we are to him. But then Jesus says to us, "OK, while you are here in this world, while you are in this less than perfect world, believe that this is not all there is. Believe that something much greater has been prepared for you. But I don't want you to go there yet. So hold on, because there is a lot more I want to do through you.

"I want you to be my church. I want you to love people. I want you to feed people who are hungry. I want you to go on walks to help people who are sick. I want you to visit people in the hospital. I want you to show up at the prisons. I want you to be there for the world.

"Above all, I want you to love. And I don't want you to love just the people who love you, but I want you to love the people who hate you as well. I want you to make the most of your mark in life. I want you to follow me. I will show you how to do this. I am the way, the truth, and the life. When it is all said and done, you will die, and because I was raised from the dead, you will be raised too. I will bring you into the kingdom of heaven forever. Where I live, you will live forever."

But until then we have some work to do. Until then we have some messes we cannot clean up, but we can tell the world who can do this. The Bible says about eternity, "What we suffer now is nothing compared with the glory that God will reveal to us. Our eyes have not seen nor have our ears heard what God has in store for us."

I know that a lot of us are hurting today. I know that this world is hurting. We have the responsibility as Christians to do everything we can to bring healing to those that are hurting. We are not called to some pie-in-the-sky theology that says, "I am going to heaven soon, so why do I have to care?" God says, "You must care for others because I care. You must love because I have loved you. I am sending you back into the world."

But eternity puts some perspective on our suffering. Our suffering here will not last forever, for heaven is eternity. Look at the life God has planned for you in eternity. What we suffer now is nothing compared to the glory God will reveal to us.

What are you living for?

Jesus says the kingdom of heaven is like a merchant who finds a precious pearl and will give up everything to hold onto it. This is what the kingdom of heaven is like. If you knew how good it is, you would give up everything else in your life to hold onto it. Are you living just for today? Or do you have an eternal perspective in your life? God wants you to love the people of this world and to be the church.

Romans 13 says it is time for us to wake up, to wake up from our spiritual slumber. It is time for us to become the people God created us to be. Jesus' death on the cross means that he shows up and takes on the enemies we cannot defeat. It means that he shows up and destroys those enemies, especially the enemy called death.

What other hope do we have beyond the grave? Someday we are going to die, and that is part of where this mess is leading. Are we going to let a real God show up in the midst of that? Are we going to let him come close to us? Are we going to let him give us the gift of eternity?

You may be thinking, "But I am not worthy of this. I just don't belong." If this is what you are thinking, look at the upper room. Look at who Jesus included at the table. He included Peter, a man who would deny him three times. He included Judas, the one who would betray him for thirty pieces of silver. He had Thomas, who seems to doubt everything that Jesus says and does.

Maybe you are like Thomas today. You say, "Oh, I am really skeptical. I really don't know if I can believe all of this. It is just pie in the sky. It is just a fairy tale. It is just not true."

That was Thomas. He said, "I am not going to play the fool. I know all the rest of the disciples are saying Jesus has risen from the dead and that they have seen him. But I'm not going to believe it until I see Jesus with my own eyes." Maybe this is you as well, the uncomfortable skeptic saying, "God, you are going to have to prove it to me."

But just at that moment, Jesus shows up and says to Thomas, "Put your hands in the holes in my hands where the nails were driven, and touch my side where the spear pierced me. See that I really was dead." And Thomas crumbles to the ground and proclaims the saving words, "My Lord and my God."

Then Jesus says something to Thomas that anyone who is skeptical needs to hear. Jesus says, "Thomas, you would be so much happier, you would be so much more blessed, if you could believe in me without seeing. You would be so much happier if you could have a relationship of faith with me rather than a relationship of proof. You would be so much happier and at peace if you could trust me."

All of the important relationships in the world are based on trust. They are all based on faith. Think about it: They are not proof-based. Proof is nice, but if you don't have trust in a relationship, it doesn't work. For those of you who are married, you know this. If you do not have trust, there is no marriage.

God wants nothing less than this, that you develop trust in him. He wants you to have faith. He wants you to have a relationship with him that is based on faith. God could prove it to you, but he doesn't act that way. Because he wants you to have faith, Jesus says to us, "I will give you plenty of evidence. I will give you plenty of signs. I will give you my word. I will tell you through me, the Living Word, that you can trust me. And you can trust that what I say will come true."

Notice that God says, "You can trust my word." It happened just the way the Bible said it would. Jesus died on the cross and rose again, and through faith we are united with Jesus Christ. We have a God who loved us enough to come down to earth for us. God loves us and the world so much that he gave us his only Son, Jesus, so that if you believe in him, you will not die but have everlasting life. You have God's word on that. "I will give you life," God says. "I will give you eternity."

About the author

Mike Housholder is senior pastor of Lutheran Church of Hope in West Des Moines, Iowa. He earned a bachelor's degree magna cum laude with a double major in English and Communication from Concordia College in Moorhead, Minnesota, in 1986, then received a Master of Divinity degree from Luther Seminary in St. Paul in 1990. After seminary training, he served as pastor at Palestine Lutheran Church in rural Huxley, Iowa.

In 1993, Housholder became the new mission developer for Lutheran Church of Hope. With a passion for fulfilling both the Great Commission and the Great Commandment, he organized the congregation upon the Bible-based vision of becoming a Spirit-filled, growing, Christ-centered community filled with hope.

As senior pastor at Hope, Housholder has surrounded himself with an exceptionally gifted core of pastors, staff, and volunteer leaders. Working in teams fueled by the Holy Spirit, Hope has completed five major building projects, launched two satellite congregations, connected thousands of people through small groups and discipleship classes, partnered with numerous local and global outreach ministries, and developed a multitude of ministries that address needs within the body of Christ.

Hope has become one of the fastest growing churches in the nation. But more important, the Holy Spirit is using Hope to bring thousands of people back to the Christian faith, teach them what it means to follow Jesus, and send them out together in mission to share God's love for the world.

In recent years, Housholder was listed in *Outreach Magazine* as one of 25 Church Leaders to Watch and received the Forty Under 40 Award from the *Des Moines Business Record*. He served on the original Core Leadership Team for Alpha USA and has been a board member for Meals from the Heartland. His sermon podcasts are downloaded by thousands of people around the world.

Housholder enjoys a variety of sports, and still holds onto the dream that he will one day win the Daytona 500 auto race or pitch for the Chicago Cubs in the World Series! He and his wife, Sally, were married in 1987 and have three children.